WRITING YOUR WAY UP THE LADDER

GAIN THAT CRITICAL ADVANTAGE
LEARN *HOW* TO MAKE
EFFECTIVE WRITING A HABIT

By David R. Gunderson

FOCUS PUBLISHING COMPANY

MICHIGAN

WRITING YOUR WAY

UP THE LADDER

Focus Publishing Company
29175 Oak Point Drive, Farmington Hills, Michigan 48018

© 1981, David R. Gunderson
Printed in the United States of America
All rights reserved.

Library of Congress Catalog Card Number: 81-67248
International Standard Book Number: 0-938442-02-3

To an inspiration.
The fountainhead of
achievement.

TABLE OF CONTENTS

PAGE

List of Tables vi

Introduction 1

Section One — Follow The Fundamentals 7

Chapter 1 — Follow The Fundamentals 9
A summary of grammar usage, parts of speech and
sentence structure
Chapter 2 — Follow The Fundamentals 27
Some simple minded mistakes and how to avoid them

Section Two — Objectives To Improve Organization 51

Chapter 3 — For Effective Writing — Focus The
Content 53
Chapter 4 — For Effective Writing — Plan The Format   61
Chapter 5 — For Effective Writing — Orchestrate The
Logic 79

Section Three — Objectives To Improve Persuasiveness ... 91

Chapter 6 — For Effective Writing — Be Absolutely
Clear............................... 93
Chapter 7 — For Effective Writing — Emphasize
Strategically 107
Chapter 8 — For Effective Writing — Select An
Appropriate Tone 117
Chapter 9 — For Effective Writing — Tailor Your Style 125
Chapter 10 — For Effective Writing — Write Efficiently 135

Section Four — Make Effective Writing A Habit 145

Chapter 11 — Make Effective Writing A Habit......... 147

Index 155

LIST OF TABLES

NUMBER	TITLE	PAGE
1	PARTS OF SPEECH	13
2	COMMON PREPOSITIONS	14
3	COMMON CONJUNCTIONS	14
4	ARTICLES	17
5	VERBALS	18
6	THOUGHT GROUPINGS	20
7	PHRASES	22
8	CLAUSES	22
9	SUBORDINATING CONNECTORS	24
10	TYPES OF SENTENCES	24
11	50 COMMON SPELLING MISTAKES	28
12	10 USEFUL SPELLING RULES	29
13	USE OF THE COMMA	32
14	USE OF THE SEMICOLON	34
15	INFLECTIONS	35
16	RULES FOR INFLECTIONS	36
17	VERB FORMS	36
18	VOICE OF VERBS	38
19	CONJUGATION OF TO BE	38
20	PERSONAL PRONOUNS	40
21	USE OF PRONOUNS	40
22	FREQUENTLY MISUSED WORDS	42

LIST OF TABLES

NUMBER	TITLE	PAGE
23	ERRORS OF OMISSION	44
24	OBJECTIVES FOR WRITING	53
25	PRINCIPLES TO FOCUS CONTENT	54
26	PRINCIPLES FOR PLANNING FORMAT	61
27	BUSINESS COMMUNICATION FORMATS	69
28	PRINCIPLES FOR LOGIC	79
29	PSYCHOLOGY OF ARGUMENT	84
30	CHARACTERISTICS OF PARAGRAPHS	86
31	STANDARD CONNECTIONS (HOOKS)	87
32	OBJECTIVES FOR ORGANIZATION	89
33	OBJECTIVES FOR PERSUASION	95
34	PRINCIPLES FOR WRITING CLEARLY	95
35	FIGURES OF SPEECH	100
36	GRAMMAR FOR CLARITY	104
37	WRITING TO CONTROL EMPHASIS	107
38	CHOICE OF TONE	117
39	PRINCIPLES FOR CONTROLLING TONE	119
40	ELEMENTS THAT CREATE INTEREST	121
41	PRINCIPLES OF STYLE	126
42	CONCEPTS THAT INDUCE CONTROL	128
43	PRINCIPLES FOR EFFICIENCY	135
44	10 COMMANDMENTS FOR GOOD WRITING HABITS	148

INTRODUCTION

A TALENT for writing is an invaluable asset. In any profession or vocation, numerous skills are prerequisites for advancement, promotion, or other recognition of successfully performing better than your peers. The one skill that stands out as being universally admired in any business discipline is the ability to convey thoughts in writing. It is a talent that is surprisingly rare, and as with any commodity, its scarcity commands a premium value.

Writing talent is rare, and yet vital, since many careers, probably most careers, involve some degree of writing. Salesmen, from those in Fortune 500's largest organizations, to those in one person enterprises, have continual requirements to express themselves in a persuasive and convincing manner. Accountants, bankers and brokers prepare reports, letters and written material to others within their companies, to clients and to associates. Managers, foremen, purchasing agents, personnel agents, secretaries and executives all originate written material — many will do so more than they ever anticipated. Lawyers, doctors, engineers, scientists and those in other professions will write to varying degrees. And regardless of how well individuals are regarded for their vocational expertise, much of the impression they convey of themselves will be dependent on how well they write.

Outstanding knowledge and ability in your vocation, without the ability to communicate your talents to others, seldom results in a successful career. An engineer may have a honed sense of creatively applying outstanding scientific knowledge to solving technical problems in his field, but he still must communicate. He or she may have mastered the use of computers, sophisticated instruments, testing devices, and the other tools-of-the-trade necessary for successful performance, but they must

1

communicate the results to others. Pure theoreticians may utilize mathematic theory to perfection or even advance the state-of-the-art and expand contemporary knowledge, but they must communicate before their ideas have value. Moreover, in today's highly organized society, knowledge is commonplace. Multitudes of "geniuses" are graduating from a myriad of educational institutions, within the business sector itself, as well as from the great citadels of higher education. Outstanding competence in your field may well eliminate much of your competition, but a great discriminator remains — the ability to communicate the results of your work to others.

Even in business fields such as marketing, advertising, or journalism, which are predominately careers in communicating to others, the ability to use the written word as a personal expression of thought is the major ingredient for one's success and another's failure. A difference exists between grinding out written material for a finished product that is not identified with the author, and original composition that remains an expression of the individual. Consider a writer for Forbes magazine. The article he or she composes will undoubtedly reflect the recognizable style of the magazine. But what of the intracompany memo that suggests the idea for the article in the first place? That is the one this book is intended to address. The latter will be more influential in the success of the writer than the former. This is so because of the individualistic nature of communicating in writing. It is a reflection of the individual and as such will constantly be used by others to evaluate the writer on a personal level.

Any experienced businessman is well aware of how few people develop the important skill of effective business writing, or appear to be cognizant of the role it plays in a successful career. All too frequently, deficiencies in writing ability are humorously discounted with an attitude of "You know what I meant." Every executive, however, is keenly aware of those in the organization that consistently provide effective written material. Those who would move up the pyramid surely would facilitate the climb by using writing ability to their advantage, rather than it being a handicap to be overcome by outstanding performance in other areas.

In 20 years of experience in business, I have a wealth of examples of ineffective writing to draw upon. Taken out of context, many are humerous, but at the time, they resulted in poor communications, misunderstandings, delays, or worse yet, poor decisions or other actions that impacted on profits. Managers spend a great deal of time and attention in evaluating, editing, or interacting in a variety of ways with the written work of those under them. Sloppy managers frequently will not make the effort (and it is an effort) to straighten out ineffectual writing, even though they know better and the document requires their own signature. Conscientious managers find their own efficiency reduced by the necessity to correct or rewrite constantly. Many employees seem to have the attitude that their job is to be sure the right thoughts are presented, and that their boss will take care of the final published form. The ones that move up the ladder, however, develop a management presence early, even before they become managers, and they do not submit their compositions until they are satisfied they would be willing to sign their own name to it, and publish it without further modification.

Even though I am a marketing executive in a large industrial firm, when asked what I do for a living, I frequently reply, "I'm a writer." It just happens that I write about the automotive industry and, presently, I write primarily about marketing issues within that industry. A few years ago my *job* required that I write about developing new products, and before that about advanced engineering matters, and before that about cost control systems. I am now in that amorphous strata referred to as middle management, neither junior, nor senior — but I have had better than average upward mobility. I know that whatever success I have achieved has been based largely on my writing ability. And I see many around me also writing their way up the ladder.

An appreciation of the importance of writing in a successful career may be obvious, but too few seem to understand what it takes to be an effective writer. They may not comprehend the objectives of writing or the means to achieve such objectives. The intended objectives of business communications are as varied as the fields of endeavor in a sophisticated society. My concept of *objectives*, however, is to define the factors that result in successfully communicating ideas in written form, regardless of the subject matter. Appropriate communication objectives reinforce the achievement of the business objectives. I believe a thorough understanding of *writing* objectives is a prerequisite for effective business communications.

In establishing my list of objectives, I searched my experience and that of others for a common thread — universal objectives that should apply to any written communications in order to get the message across most effectively. While others might devise a somewhat different list, or emphasize other characteristics, I know if the people that have worked for me over the years had only met the writing objectives outlined in this book, their performance would have been immeasurably improved.

Following the fundamentals of good English composition is essential in achieving effectiveness. Therefore, it is my first objective. Spelling, punctuation, sentence structure, vocabulary, and accepted grammar are the means by which the objectives described in this book are literally fulfilled. Clarity, order, emphasis, tone and style are all transmitted (or not) through the use of basic English fundamentals. Yet it is not the intent here to educate the reader on such fundamentals. It is assumed my audience has had full exposure to the use of English — if not, the reader is encouraged to take full advantage of the opportunity to take every course possible in English, literature and related subjects, regardless of his intended vocation, as necessary preparation for effective business communications.

Effective writing, however, requires more than a mastery of such fundamentals. Effective organization and persuasive presentation of the writer's thoughts are also required. Therefore, the second section of this book discusses three basic writing objectives inherent in effective organization — to focus the content, to plan the format and to orchestrate the logic. The third section of the book deals with five basic objectives for persuasive writing — clarity, emphasis, tone, style and efficiency. The last chapter gives the reader my ten commandments for making effective writing habitual.

In numerous hours of research while preparing this book, it was apparent that hundreds have attempted to convey the fundamentals of English to their readers. Teachers predominately write such books, usually for students at various levels of education, or for aspiring novelists. They usually emphasize grammatical rules, the dos and don'ts of the parts of speech, punctuation and construction. Many include detailed explanations of the preferred format for essays, reports, term papers, thesises, or business letters. A few elaborate on writing style. The classic, of course, in this regard, is the "little book", *The Elements of Style*, by Strunk and White (MacMillan). Another I liked, was *The Lively Art Of Writing*, by Lucile Payne (Mentor), although it was primarily oriented toward writing an essay. Edward Newman, the correspondent (one of the few outside of the teaching profession to tackle the subject), took a different approach in his book *Strictly Speaking*. He avoided stating dry rules and instead buried the reader in a torrent of abuse and misuse of the language that left me, for one, laughing days later.

I found no books written by businessmen, those in a position to perhaps offer the best advice, on effective business communications. The advice that I believe is missing has to do with certain unique aspects of business correspondence that require emphasizing different elements of writing techniques, although such techniques are universally applied in all fields. For example, numerous books instruct budding novelists to write for themselves, not for their unknown readers, as the most successful way to create art. Businessmen also must develop their own writing style, but the purpose of their correspondence is usually well defined and focused to a known audience. Business writers also must understand and emphasize formatting techniques, tone considerations, and methods of persuasion from a different perspective. Businessmen can emulate the fundamentals of logical organization practiced by essayists, but the business context also induces unique considerations. Therefore, while much of the advice in this book is common to that given for effective writing in all fields, it is approached from the vantage point of specifically producing effective business correspondence.

Even though it seemed perilous for me to venture into the domain of the educators, I took heart knowing that much of a manager's existence is devoted to training subordinates — educating them, if you will. If this book is to have value, then, it should be interpreted not as a profound scholastic writing manual, but rather as the practical advice of an active, successful businessman and a helpful reference book for use "on the job".

The elements of effective business writing are not mysterious nor unfamiliar. Elementary concepts of creative writing, construction and grammar are required. The precepts are taught to us all from the earliest levels of grade school, through college graduate courses. The English language is a beautiful and fascinating medium to convey every nuance of thought. The premise for this book is that ineffective writing is primarily a matter of a lack of understanding of the writing objectives that determine the success or failure of the communication. A recognition of such objectives is necessary before a thoughtful person can apply the full power of the written word to business communications. Regardless of the vocation, one who masters this skill will gain an important tool with which to compete more successfully.

SECTION ONE

FOLLOW THE FUNDAMENTALS

1

FOLLOW THE FUNDAMENTALS

PARTS OF SPEECH AND SENTENCE STRUCTURE

FEW BUSINESSMEN today have had the benefit of sufficient educational background in writing. Early in my career, I had the good fortune to work for an English teacher who changed his vocation to an automotive engineer as a result of a glut in the teachers' job market years before. With his English background, he would enjoy nothing better than finding a young engineer's participle dangling. If I wrote, "Having taken the measurements, the results are obvious," he would sarcastically add to the margin, "The results are not as obvious as your dangle!", leaving me perplexed as to what on earth was wrong now. I soon dog-eared page 284 of my *Harbrace* for the chapter on *Dangling Modifiers*, which I still have occasion to refer to, even though I no longer have the same boss and I now can recognize most dangling situations.

Some managers develop a fetish concerning a few grammatical errors, many times as a substitute for a more comprehensive understanding of all elements of good writing. Although my former boss in engineering could not be accused of having a fetish about dangling modifiers, since he was equally quick to edit any grammatical errors (even to the extent of using conventional editing symbols, which we all learned to recognize), I have found that many executives have a particular hang-up about certain grammatical errors. Even when in deep concentration while reading the text, the error will leap out at them, disrupt their train of thought, and bring out the sting of the red felt-tip pen. One manager, for whom I would write papers that he would then present to the Executive Committee, urged that the text be written so that it would read as if he were in a normal conversation. But whoa unto me if I casually left out articles. I can see it now . . .

Emphasizing similar traits of Arrow and Spade programs, exaggerates differences to our advantage.

Other managers had fetishes about spelling errors (commonly referred to as *typos*), or the use of commas (too many, or too few), or the intermixing of tense forms (amo, amas, amat). The highly unusual case, like the former English teacher-engineer, puts it all together. Rather than firing for effect (or is it affect), by concentrating on a few familiar errors, such a person consistently strives for following the fundamentals of the proper use of the English language in all respects. It's this last manager, the perfectionist, who is most likely to stand out and be recognized as a *good writer*. By so doing, he will have gained an advantage in the race to the top.

The first objective for anyone interested in writing their way up the ladder is to follow the fundamentals. Several good reasons for this come to mind, other than to impress your superiors and to intimidate your subordinates. In the first place, writing is a reflection of the personality holding the pen. One who follows the fundamentals without compromise projects an image of intelligence and diligence in attention to detail. More than that, this shows a respect for the reader. It is a mistake to assume the reader does not care, or will understand that a minor error is not worth the time it will take to correct it. Such an approach merely projects a careless mind at best, or worse, a disregard for the reader's intelligence. If the writer believes the text is important enough to be read, he owes it to the reader to accept that it is important enough to write correctly in the first place.

Equally as important as conveying a positive image of the writer to his audience, the use of accepted grammar is important in achieving the primary purpose of putting pen to paper in the first place — the objective of clearly communicating your thoughts to the reader. The rules of grammar are all directed toward this end. Unlike oral communications, which benefit greatly from supporting facial expressions, gestures, or sound inflections, written communications are self-contained ex-pressions of thought. The choice of words, the punctuation, the sentence structure, and the organization of the sentences and paragraphs all must work together to represent exactly what the writer had in mind.

The difficulty in applying the obviously sensible objective of following the fundamentals in a business environment is the wide variety of demands for written communications in the nor-mal, day-in, day-out affairs of an office. The vast majority of businessmen may not be well versed in the fundamentals, but worse yet, only a small minority worry about using correct grammar, unless the communication has the status of an annual report. The press of business, they believe, is too demanding on their time to dally over the niceties of grammar. Again, it's the "You know what I mean" syndrome. Then too, communications actually do vary in importance depending on whether it's an informal note within the office, a memo to file, a letter to an outsider, a progress report, a tightly woven argument leading to a recommendation, or a formal presentation to the Board of Direc-tors.

The solution to this apathy is to recognize the importance that written communications (of every type) play in a successful career, and secondly, to master the fundamentals so that good writing is habitual. After all, the fundamentals are not that difficult and with some effort early in your career, you will find it easier and even quicker to write effectively by utilizing correct grammar in all correspondence.

What, then, are these *fundamentals*? The libraries are full of volumes on this subject ranging from beginners' primers to very complex and detailed books that are enough to discourage even the more stalwart student of the subject. This chapter will attempt to summarize certain elements of all that could be said on this subject. The elements chosen are sufficient to handle normal business correspondence so that this chapter can be used as a reference source, or working tool, for the active businessman.

First, an aside. *Grammar* is the study of words forming the parts of speech, their inflections, and their functions and rela-tions in the sentence. *Grammatically correct* refers to con-formance with the rules of grammar — and yet no rigid rules exist, only accepted practices. The English language is a fluid medium of communication that is ever evolving. For instance, *data* is generally regarded as a plural noun, never to be used with singular verbs. You should never write "The data is . . . ," but rather "The data are. . ." And yet, more and more, *data* is used in business correspondence to refer to a singular group of facts, rather than individual things, and the plurality of data frequently seems awkward. Here is a word in transition, and it is predictable that the purists will soon be left with an archaic grammatical form. Transitions in grammatical acceptance lead to much of the confusion regarding the use of good grammar.

The test for proper usage is always the ear. Write the way you speak. Reread your writing to yourself and rewrite, if necessary, until you would feel comfortable standing in front of the recipient reading it. If you lack sufficient education to have mastered the fundamentals, that's tough — you are what you are, and your writing will be less effective if you try to use an unnatural or stilted style. Even with extensive time and effort to learn the fundamentals, occasions will arise when the grammatically correct sentence does not sound right. In cases like that, learn to trust your ear. Rewrite until it has the right ring to it.

With proper training, however, you can develop an ear for normally accepted grammar. Usually you will find that when a sentence or paragraph bothers you, it will be because the fundamentals were not adhered to. Therefore, my best advice when a *rewrite* appears to be necessary is to go back to the basics, look for mistakes in the fundamentals and rewrite or reconstruct the thought using normally accepted grammar.

Now let's refresh your memory regarding the fundamentals of English grammar. Before it is possible to understand grammatical mistakes, to spot them and correct them, or to avoid them, it is mandatory to understand the parts of speech and the fundamentals of sentence structure.

PARTS OF SPEECH

There are only 8 parts of speech (shown in Table 1). All words fall under one of the eight categories, although many words may be used in several of the categories depending on their usage in a sentence.

I will *fast* until the holidays are over. (Verb)

The mare galloped *fast*. (Adverb — modifying galloped)

This is a *fast* mare. (Adjective — modifying mare)

Table 1

PARTS OF SPEECH

1. Verb	Indicators of action or state of being.
2. Noun	Subjects, objects, or complements.
3. Pronoun	Substitution for nouns.
4. Adjective	Modifiers of nouns.
5. Adverb	Modifiers of verbs, adjectives, or adverbs.
6. Conjunction	Connectives.
7. Preposition	Words used before nouns to connect them to other words in the sentence.
8. Interjection	Expressions of emotion (alas!).

Identifying parts of speech is important solely to determine the appropriate order of words in a sentence and the necessary punctuation to express a thought. A *sentence* is a sequence of words that expresses a complete thought — a thought that requires no further amplification to have meaning. The most simple sentence consists of a *subject*, represented by a noun, and a *predicate*, represented by a verb:

> I ran. (Although an implied subject would be written even simpler: "Run!")

The verb connotes action. To find the subject, simply ask *who* or *what* acted (or was acted upon). Without a verb, a series of words is not a sentence, but a fragment.

The next degree of complexity involves an *object* of the sentence — a noun or pronoun that receives the action of the verb. Word sequence within a sentence is the only means for differentiating whether a noun is being used as a subject or an object:

> Standard Form:
> Subject-Verb-Object.

> Consider the following:
> The man killed the woman. or,
> The woman killed the man.

You had better believe it is important to the man and the woman involved which sequence they come in within the sentence.

Table 2

COMMON PREPOSITIONS

across	between	in front of	to
after	by	in regard to	together with
as	for	of	under
at	from	on	up
before	in	over	with

Table 3

COMMON CONJUNCTIONS

Coordinating	Subordinating		Conjunctive Adverbs
and	although	after	however
but	as	because	therefore
or, either	in order that	if	nevertheless
nor, neither	unless	since	hence
for	before	till	then
so	until	when	besides
yet	whenever	where	moreover
	wherever	which	accordingly
	than		thus
			otherwise
			consequently

Adjectives and *adverbs* are words that modify other words, but relate to expanding the basic three-part sentence structure to allow for more specific thoughts. Adjectives describe nouns. Adverbs indicate time, place, manner, or degree.

> The *angry* (adjective) man *almost* (adverb) killed the *repeatedly* (adverb) *unfaithful* (adjective) woman.

The remainder of the parts of speech (*pronouns, prepositions and conjunctions*) are useful to allow for amplification of the basic thought.

> *In* (preposition) the morning, the angry man almost killed the repeatedly unfaithful woman, *but* (conjunction) shot *himself* (pronoun) instead.

Prepositions are words that are used with nouns to connect the nouns to the rest of the sentence and usually connote time, place or identification. Examples of frequently used prepositions are shown in Table 2. The preposition *to* is probably the most overworked little word in the language and more will be said about *to* later in the book.

Conjunctions are words that are used to connect phrases or clauses to the main part of the sentence. Depending on the word used, the conjunction can give the related thought an equal status to the main sentence (a coordinating conjunction) or a secondary status (a subordinating conjunction). Conjunctive adverbs are also used to connect thoughts, however, they are connectives between main thoughts only. Examples of words used as conjunctions are shown in Table 3. We must discuss conjunctions in more detail later as well.

We can see from the foregoing example that all of the parts of speech are necessary to effectively communicate a total thought. We went from the woman being killed, to almost being killed, to the man being killed (or at least shot). Only the writer knew the facts, and it is important to note there were many ways for him to combine words into sentences to convey what happened. The way he selected *sounded* right to him. Now we begin to understand why writing is an expression of the individual. Another writer in describing the same scene may have elected to be more verbose, or use different adjectives, or different verbs to express more vivid emotions or actions. No single rule exists to guide the writer, and yet, one writer can be immeasurably more effective than another. The bulk of this book will be devoted to understanding this phenomena, but first we must slog through a few more fundamentals.

All of the foregoing is complicated one degree further by the fact that groups of words can be combined into *phrases* and *clauses* that can be used as parts of speech and, also, to develop compound subjects (nouns) or predicates (verbs).

She and I (compound subject) *laughed and sang* (compound predicate) all night.

Phrases and clauses deserve a separate discussion since their use and misuse are key to effective writing, and many fundamental mistakes can be avoided through a better understanding of phrases and clauses. First, however, let's dismiss with four other grammatical forms that are equally important to understand.

ARTICLES, PARTICIPLES, GERUNDS, AND INFINITIVES AS PARTS OF SPEECH

Four other definitions are necessary to complete the picture relative to parts of speech. The first is for the *ARTICLES* — the, a, and an (Table 4). As my former boss taught me, articles are necessary adjectives that can be left out only at the risk of ambiguity:

The man killed . . .	Identifies a known man.
A man killed . . .	The sex of the killer is known, but not his identity.

Table 4

ARTICLES ARE NECESSARY ADJECTIVES

Definite Article	Indefinite Article
The	A, An

Justification never exists for leaving articles out, or worse, using them at random:

A noun is used as *a* subject or (*an*) object.

The superintendent had to terminate *the* foreman, *the* drill press operator and (*the*) maintenance man.

Table 5

VERBALS

Used to connect thoughts to the main sentence.

Participles	Gerunds	Infinitives
• Used as adjectives	• Used as nouns	• Used as nouns, adjectives, or adverbs
• Derived from verbs by adding a different ending to the base word	• Derived from verbs by adding "-ing" to base word	• Derived from verbs by adding the word "to" in front of the base word

Present Participle:

• Ends in "-ing"
Example: "The <u>working</u> man . . ."

Past Participle:

• Ends in -ed, -d, -t, -en, -n, or changes base word

Example: "The <u>written</u> word . . ."

Example: "The <u>drunk</u> man . . ."

• Identified by usage in the sentence; never used to modify another word.

Example: "<u>Working</u> is . . ."

• Tense determined by form of base verb

Present Tense:

Example: "<u>To write</u> is a skill."

Past Tense:

Example: "<u>To have written</u> such a thing was careless."

Future Tense:

Example: "The book has <u>to be written</u>."

Participles, gerunds and *infinitives* are words, or groups of words derived from verbs, and hence referred to as "verbals." They are similar to each other in the sense they are used to connect thoughts to the main sentence; however, they are quite different in the way they are used within the total sentence. A summary of how each verbal is derived from a base verb and the use of each verbal is shown in Table 5.

PARTICIPLES are used as adjectives, i.e., to modify nouns only. Verbs, of course, have a tense — either past, present, or future (also past perfect, present perfect, or future perfect). Participles are no different. Actually, the most frequent grammatical mistake related to the use of a participle is when its tense is inconsistent with the tense of the verb used in the sentence (except for the mistaken use of a participle phrase as a complete sentence, when it is always a fragment). The present participle is formed by adding *-ing* to the base verb. The past participle is formed normally by adding common past tense endings to the verb, with its place in the sentence determining whether it is being used as a verb or past participle. For *irregular* verbs, the past participle is formed by changes to the base word, i.e., drink, drank, drunk.

Disagreement in tense:
  Working at a fast pace, the man *was* tired.

Agreement in tense:
  Having worked at a fast pace, the man *was* tired.

GERUNDS are verb forms used as nouns and are always formed by adding *-ing* to the base verb. They are only distinguishable from their twin, present participle, by their usage in the sentence:

Gerund:
  Working is fun. (Noun, subject)

  Careless working is dangerous. (Noun phrase, subject)

Table 6

THOUGHT GROUPINGS

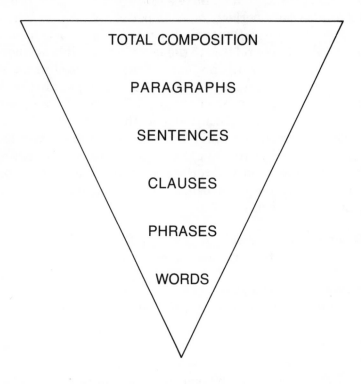

TOTAL COMPOSITION

PARAGRAPHS

SENTENCES

CLAUSES

PHRASES

WORDS

   INFINITIVES are the most versatile of the three verbal forms. They can be used as nouns, adjectives or adverbs, which helps to explain why they are prevalent in normal writing. As with participles, it is important to obtain agreement between the verb tense in the sentence and the tense of the verbal forming the infinitive.

   Infinitive as a noun:
      To eat too much can be fattening. (Subject)

   Infinitive as a noun:
      The solution is *to recognize* . . . (Object)

   Infinitive as an adjective:
      Writers have a responsibility *to write accurately*. (Modifies responsibility)

   Infinitive as an adverb:
      The writer prayed *to gain success*. (Modifies prayed)

   We mentioned earlier the use of the preposition *to* as a common connector for adding words in relation to the rest of the sentence. Such prepositional phrases are not to be confused with the infinitive form. The difference is that the infinitive combines *to* with a verb, whereas the preposition *to* does not.

      The river flowed *to the sea*. (Prepositional phrase)

      The man screamed *to shake his fear*. (Infinitive phrase)

PHRASES, CLAUSES, AND SENTENCES
   English grammar can be thought of as a logical way to group ideas into a hierarchy of expression or understanding. A single word generates an individual thought and the thought expands as words are combined in a meaningful way (Table 6).
   Just as individual words, as well as the foregoing verbal forms, are used to form the eight basic parts of speech, groups of words are combined into related thoughts to form *phrases* that are also used as nouns, adjectives, or adverbs. Such phrases are incomplete thoughts that have neither subject, nor predicate, and are connected to the rest of the sentence to complete the thought. Groups of words that *do* have a subject and predicate are called *clauses*. Clauses may stand alone as complete sentences, or be connected to a main clause with a subordinating connecting word

Table 7

PHRASES

Do not contain subject and predicate.

Types

Determined by connecting (first) word:

- Prepositional phrase
- Participle phrase
- Gerund phrase
- Infinitive phrase

Table 8

CLAUSES

Contain subject and predicate (verb).

Types

- Main clause — thought stands alone as a complete sentence.

- Subordinate clause — cannot stand alone; used as noun, adjective or adverb.

that relates the subordinate clause to the main clause. The combination of individual words, phrases, and clauses with appropriate punctuation results in the sentence form — the fundamental thought group that can make complete sense without additional explanation. But sentences can be combined into paragraphs to broaden the thought and paragraphs into total compositions as the writer communicates his total message.

The fundamental concept of thinking of a *hierarchy of thought groupings* is useful both in terms of the broad logic of communication and in terms of remembering the basic grammatical rules of sentence structure and punctuation. Writing is a matter of interrupting an unending stream of thoughts emanating from the brain of the writer and selecting the thoughts that pertain to the communication. The organization and order and logic of collecting these largely disjointed thoughts into an effective communication is the essence of the thought grouping concept.

PHRASES are the first order of thought grouping, when a single word is not sufficiently explanatory. Phrases can be subjects (nouns) or modifiers (adjectives or adverbs), and may be introduced or connected to the sentence by either a participle or any of the three verbals (Table 7).

Example	Phrase Type	Usage
• Phrases must be connected *to the sentence*.	Prepositional	Noun, object
• *Having defined phrases*, we can move on.	Participle	Adjective, modifies we
• *Writing a book* is hard work.	Gerund	Noun, subject
• *To recognize a phrase*, is important.	Infinitive	Noun, subject
• We are now prepared *to understand* clauses.	Infinitive	Adverb, modifies prepared

CLAUSES are either independent thoughts, which could stand alone as complete sentences, or dependent thoughts that are subordinate to the main clause (Table 8). Subordinate clauses are identified (and actually formed) by the fact that they are

Table 9

SUBORDINATING CONNECTORS

- Subordinating conjunction
  (unless, after, while, etc.)

- Relative pronouns
  (who, whom, which, what, that, whoever)

Table 10

TYPES OF SENTENCES

- Simple sentence — a single main clause.

- Compound sentence — two, or more, main clauses.

- Complex sentence — one main clause and at least
  one subordinate clause.

- Compound-complex sentence — two, or more, main clauses
  and at least one subordinate clause.

introduced with a subordinating conjunction (the sixth part of speech, remember) or a relative pronoun (Table 9).

Now that we can recognize the difference between a phrase and a clause, and further, know the difference between a main clause and a subordinate clause, we are prepared to readily understand the four classifications of sentence structure (Shown in Table 10).

Sentence Type	Example
• Simple sentence	Sentences fall under four classifications.
• Compound sentence	Every sentence has one main clause, *and* a compound sentence has at least two.
• Complex sentence	A sentence may have two clauses, *although* one may be subordinate to the other.
• Compound-complex sentence	Recognizing sentence structure is not difficult, *and* it is necessary for proper punctuation, *unless* the writer is ignorant.

We began this brief discussion of fundamentals by describing the basic element of expressing a total thought — a simple sentence has the form: subject-verb-object. All of the rest of the discussion pertains to how the other parts of speech and elemental groupings of words can be used to expand this simple sentence into the most complex total self-contained thought — the compound-complex sentence, which with supporting phrases can be as long as the writer chooses. Although far from being a complete summary of grammar fundamentals, this discussion should be a sufficient refresher for those with previous exposure to English composition to proceed with the next section regarding fundamentals — a collection of common, if not the most frequent, grammatical errors in business writing.

2

FOLLOW THE FUNDAMENTALS

SOME SIMPLE MINDED MISTAKES

BEING WELL versed in the fundamentals of good grammar, as outlined in the previous chapter, is not an end in itself, but a means to an end. Clarity of communication is the goal. This chapter illuminates the most common mistakes related to incorrect grammatical form that undermine the effectiveness of any given communication in achieving this goal. They may be referred to as "simple minded mistakes" because correct usage of the fundamentals involves simple concepts. Many reasons may exist for making careless mistakes, but few excuses can be made for making mistakes out of ignorance. This chapter will cover both types in the hope of encouraging the reader to develop a sensitivity to recognizing and correcting such mistakes.

1. SPELLING MISTAKES MISTAKENLY DISTRACT THE READER.

Spelling mistakes will undermine the effectiveness of the most carefully thought out written material. Somehow the credibility of the total effort is destroyed for most readers if they discover a spelling error. In other cases, the error changes the meaning of the word and results in confusion or ambiguity. Every writer should be constantly on guard against spelling mistakes and develop the habit of thoroughly searching for errors before the writing is considered finished. Essentially, four mistakes occur — the first are simple, careless transpositions of letters or mistakes of the "i before e, except after c" variety; the second, which are more difficult to spot, are those that involve the many spelling *rules* for word endings, inflections, or derivatives of a base word; the third result from inaccurate pronunciation of a word and a phonetic spelling mistake; the fourth result from incorrect word usage versus the intended meaning (advice, advise).

Table 11

50 COMMON SPELLING MISTAKES

Improper Usage	Improper Spelling	
a, an	apparent	maintenance
accept, except	acceptable	noticeable
advise, advice	advantageous	occasion
affect, effect	alleviate	occurrence
already, all ready	analyze	particular
can, may	belief	performance
compare to, compare with	category	permanent
continual, continuous	committee	precede
council, counsel	conscious	prevalent
devise, device	consistency	procedure
infer, imply	dependent	prominent
personel, personnel	description	referring
principal, principle	disastrous	separate
there, their	existence	similar
to, too	experience	sincerely
	guaranteed	success
	importance	warrant
	indefinite	

(The above words are spelled correctly; the underlined letters are the ones usually misspelled.)

Many books are available that are devoted to spelling. I have seen numerous lists of "most frequently misspelled words." I, for one, have great difficulty in remembering the many rules related to spelling — there seem to be so many exceptions. For the fun of it, I have included my favorite "Top 50" misspelled words (Table 11) used frequently in business correspondence and, also, my "10 Most Useful" spelling rules (Table 12). However, no matter how many lists you study, your best defense is to be well read. Even though you may not be sure how to spell a word, if you read enough, you are more likely to recognize words on sight and spot when they look *funny*. Vociferous readers are seldom poor spellers. Sight recognition also tends to avoid the phonetic mistakes that are particularly troublesome. Beyond that advice, I would suggest it is simply foolhardy not to keep a good dictionary handy and refer to it constantly.

Table 12

10 USEFUL SPELLING RULES

Some Exceptions

1. Put i before e, except after c, or when sounded like a, as in neighbor or weigh.
   foreign, height, efficient, forfeit, ancient, sufficient, leisure, financier, difficient

2. Use "ain" following t, and "ian" following d, l, and c: (certain, median, familiar, physician).
   villain

3. Dis is a complete prefix, des combines the prefix de- with the first letter of a word beginning with s: (disagree, describe).

4. Letters are never added or deleted from prefixes: (disappear, not dissappear; immortal, not imortal).

5. If a y ending is preceded by a vowel, the y is retained when adding a suffix: (obeyed).
   say, said
   pay, paid
   lay, laid
   day, daily

(continued on next page)

Table 12

10 USEFUL SPELLING RULES (Continued)

Some Exceptions

6. If a y ending is preceded by a consonant, y is changed to i, unless the suffix starts with i: (history, historical; fly, flying).

shy, shyness
spry, spryly
lady, ladylike
baby, babyhood

7. Drop the final e only before a suffix beginning with a vowel: (come, coming; care, careful; desire, desirable).

due, duly
notice, noticeable
courage, courageous
mile, mileage
wise, wisdom
argue, argument

8. Double the final consonant only if the suffix begins with a vowel and the consonant is preceded by a single vowel *and* the accent is on the last syllable of the word (or in a single syllable word): plan, planning: need, needed; begin, beginning; benefit, benefiting).

Defer, deference
confer, conference
picnic, picnicking

9. Never double the final consonant in words ending with two consonants: (skill, skilled; confirm, confirming).

Drop final consonant if a triple letter would result: (dull, dully).

10. Form the plural by adding s to the singular word, but add es if the plural makes an extra syllable: (dog, dogs; catch, catches).

Nouns ending in:
y — same as rules 5 and 6 above
fe — change fe to ve and add s.
o — if preceded by vowel, always add s.

2. IMPROPER PUNCTUATION IMPROPERLY CREATES READER CONFUSION.

Written communications are almost totally dependent on punctuation to replace the supplemental sights and sounds that accompany oral communications. A pause for effect, inflections of the voice for emphasis or a separation of thought, even gestures are all conveyed in writing through punctuation. Improper use of punctuation leads to misunderstandings and confusion. Such mistakes are probably the most frequent errors in business writing and the greatest cause of secretarial headaches as well.

Some reminders of the most common form of punctuation errors are as follows:

- The colon (:) always should be used with the meaning "as follows". The punctuation following a colon is particularly troublesome if it involves a list of items. The thing to remember is to be consistent. If the list is one of phrases, make them all phrases with common tense, and either end each with a comma or use neither commas nor periods. If clauses are used, make each item a complete sentence or use a consistent clause form.

- Use exclamation marks (!) and question marks (?) sparingly. The former because the proper choice of words can be just as effective and less distractive ("What's he getting so excited about?"); and the latter because the writer tends to lose control.

Weak:
   Would you please send the quotes by August?
(What if the answer is no?)

Better control:
   I need your quotes by August.

Table 13

COMMON "RULES" FOR USE OF THE COMMA

Rule	Example
• Separate items in a series, including before the conjunction preceding the last item.	Writing involves proper spelling, punctuation, and grammar. (Note: Last comma may be omitted if meaning is clear, such as this example.)
• Separate coordinate adjectives.	The careful, thoughtful writer does best.
• Separate main clauses joined by *and, but, or, nor, or for.*	The writer wrote well, and the results showed it.
• Separate introductory clauses or phrases from main clause (do not separate an adverb clause *following* a main clause unless it is non-restrictive*).	If a pause is necessary, consider a comma. Commas must be used *according to the rules of grammar.* (restrictive) Commas can be overused, *particularly if the meaning is clear without them.* (non-restrictive)
• Separate non-restrictive* clauses and phrases and other parenthetical elements.	Punctuation errors, such as the use of commas, are frequently made. However, rules are made to be broken.

*The concept of restrictive versus non-restrictive must be understood. If the phrase, clause, or word can be left out without altering the meaning of the sentence, it is non-restrictive.

One frequently encountered mistake is the use of a comma before "that" rather than "which".
    That — Restrictive pronoun (no comma)
    Which — Non-restrictive pronoun (use comma)

2. IMPROPER PUNCTUATION (continued)

- Dashes (--, double are better to avoid confusion with hyphens) can be effectively used as a major interruptor, but become less effective if overused. Usually a semicolon (;) is sufficient. Always question when dashes are used more than once in the same piece of correspondence.

- Parenthesis ( ) are very useful to set off supplementary or illustrative material extraneous to the main sentence. Here again, the caution is to use this form sparingly. Always question whether the timing for interjecting the thought is appropriate, or whether it could be made with normal sentence structure. Too many parenthesis are usually a sign of sloppy thought and organization.

- Commas (,) are the most misused form of punctuation, either through overuse or underuse. Five basic *rules* are shown in Table 13. Other common rules apply to geographical names, dates, footnotes and other composition details, which can be found in any good grammar book. The test is to listen to what you have written. If a pause is necessary, consider a comma. The meaning can vary considerably:

Harry, the manager was fired.
Harry, the manager, was fired.

Was Harry fired or not?

2. IMPROPER PUNCTUATION (continued)

- Semicolons (;) are frequently used in error interchange-
  ably with commas. It may be helpful to remember that
  semicolons are only used to separate elements of a sentence that have equal rank. The most common *rules* for
  proper use of semicolons are shown in Table 14.

Table 14

COMMON "RULES" FOR USE OF THE SEMICOLON

Rule	Example
• Separate two main clauses not joined by "and, but, a, nor, or for."	The river was swift; the men strained against the current.
• Separate two main clauses if the second clause is introduced with a conjunctive adverb.	The river was swift; however, the men kept their feet.
• Separate coordinate, equal elements that themselves contain commas (or required for clarity).	Semicolons are used for point one, regardless of what you think; for point two, which is easier to understand; and for point three, which is only sensible.

The foregoing briefly summarizes the most common punctuation usage. However, a good grammar book is as necessary as
a dictionary for the desk of any businessman interested in improving the effectiveness of his writing through proper punctuation.

3. INCONSISTENT INFLECTIONS REQUIRE READER REFLECTIONS.

Frequently when you catch yourself rereading a sentence or paragraph several times because the meaning is not registering, it will be because the writer has unwittingly mixed the inflections of related words. Inflections are modifications of base words to change their meaning, as when forming a plural of a noun or altering the tense of a verb. A summary of the various inflections is shown in Table 15.

Table 15

INFLECTIONS

(Connote case, gender, number, tense, person, mood or voice.)

Declensions

Conjugations

Verbs

Noun Forms

Case:	Subject/Object	Possessive
Singular:	Base word	Add 's
Plural:	Base word	Add s'

Tense	Irregular Verb
Present (present action)	I see / we see
Past (past action)	I saw / we saw
Future (action after the present)	I shall see / you will see
Present Perfect (past action extending to the present)	I have seen / we have seen
Past Perfect (past action completed)	I had seen / we had seen
Future Perfect (action to be completed)	I shall have seen / we shall have seen / you will have seen

Common Pronoun Forms

Case:	Subject	Object	Possessive
Singular			
1st Person	I	me	my, mine
2nd Person	you	you	your, yours
3rd Person	he, she, it	him, her, it	his, hers, its
Plural			
1st Person	we	us	our, ours
2nd Person	you	you	your, yours
3rd Person	they	them	their, theirs

Comparisons

Adjective, Adverb

Adjectives		Adverbs	
Positive (singular)	Good, high	**Positive**	Well, highly
Comparative (between two)	Better, higher	**Comparative**	Better, more highly
Superlative (for 3 or more)	Best, highest	**Superlative**	Best, most highly

---

Table 16

COMMON "RULES" FOR INFLECTIONS

- The verb should agree in number with the subject.

- The pronoun should agree in number with its antecedent.

- Shifts in tense should be avoided.

- Comparisons should agree in number with subjective forms and always be complete.

Table 17

VERB FORMS

	Used For	Regular	Irregular
• Present stem (infinitive)	Present Tense	ask	see
• Past tense	Past Tense	asked	saw
• Future tense	Future Tense	asked	shall see
• Past participle	All Perfect Tenses	asked	seen

Changes in the inflections of nouns or pronouns are called *declensions*. They involve changing the *case* of a word used either as the subject of the sentence, the object of the sentence, or used in the possessive form. Secondly, either the singular form or plural form of the basic word can be used. For *nouns*, the subject and object forms are the same, and the possessive is simply formed by either adding ('s) to the singular noun, or (s') to the plural noun. *Pronouns* are somewhat more involved, depending on whether the writer is referring to the first person, second person, or third person. Several common pronoun declensions are also shown in Table 15.

Common *rules* involving the proper use of inflections are shown in Table 16. The most common mistake is to have disagreement in number between the nouns, pronouns, and verbs in the same sentence.

> A man writes . . .
> The men write . . .

This sounds easier than it really is, because many sentences become quite involved. Compound subjects, compound subjects that contain a singular noun and a plural noun (Harry and the boys), parenthetical expressions that separate the subject from the verb, collective nouns (the entire office), and pronouns remotely located from their antecedent all confuse the issue. It is sufficient in this book to caution the reader about this common grammatical mistake. If achieving agreement results in awkward reading, it is best to reconstruct the sentence to avoid the problem.

Another frequent mistake is to shift the tense of the verb in a compound sentence or a paragraph, resulting in an awkward sentence or illogical meaning. The average reader is trained to recognize the difference in tense and such a shift is distracting, if not actually erroneous. As shown in Table 17, regular verbs change their tense by simply adding -ed or -d to the base; however, many irregular verb conjugations must be memorized for the proper form.

Shift:
> The recommendation *involves* complex marketing considerations and when *it would be best to spend* the money.

Table 18

VOICE OF VERBS

Active	Passive*
Verb causes subjects to act.	Verb requires action upon the subject.
I see	I am seen
You will see	You will be seen
He saw	He was seen

*Formed by adding the appropriate tense and form of "to be" with the past participle of another verb.

Table 19

CONJUGATION OF TO BE

Present Tense	Past	Past Participle	Present Participle
Be	Been	Been	Being

	Present Tense	Past Tense	Future Tense
1st Person	I am	I was	I shall be
2nd Person	you are	you were	you will be
3rd Person	he is	he was	he will be
Plural	they are	there were	they will be
	we are	we were	we shall be

	Present Perfect	Past Perfect	Future Perfect
1st Person	I have been	I had been	I shall have been
2nd Person	you have been	you had been	you will have been
3rd Person	he has been	he had been	he will have been
Plural	they have been	they had been	they will have been
	we have been	we had been	we shall have been

Inflection mistakes involving the use of adjectives or adverbs *for comparison* are less frequently made but are glaring when encountered. It is wise whenever comparisons are made to first question the number of items being compared and, equally important, double check to be sure the comparison is complete.

Riding a subway to work is better. (Than what?)

It is best to drink slowly. (Out of how many alternative ways to drink?)

By combining inflections of two verbs used together, the important concept of *voice* is produced. Because of its importance in effective writing, a separate discussion is required later in the book on *voice*. Verbs can connote either an *active voice* or a *passive voice*. As shown in Table 18, the passive voice is formed by adding the appropriate tense and form of the verb "to be," with the past participle of another verb (Table 19). The active voice is used when the subject acts and the passive voice when the subject is acted upon.

The foreman *fired* the worker. (Active)

The worker *was fired* by the foreman. (Passive)

In terms of effective communication, the active voice has more impact and more will be said of this tool in later chapters. However, in terms of following the fundamentals, it is important for the writer to correctly use the necessary voice to form a logical sentence. Frequently, there is a double mistake of shifting the subject along with a change in voice.

The speaker hurried to the podium, and the glass of water was spilled all over him. (Awkward, unclear — who spilled the water?)

The speaker hurried to the podium, and spilled the glass of water all over himself. (Consistent and clear.)

Table 20

PERSONAL PRONOUNS

Singular

	Subjective	Possessive	Objective	RELATIVE PRONOUNS
1st Person	I	my, mine	me	who
2nd Person	you	your, yours	you	which
3rd Person	he, she, it	his, her, hers, its	him, her, it	what

Plural

	Subjective	Possessive	Objective	RELATIVE PRONOUNS
1st Person	we	our, ours	us	whom
2nd Person	you	your, yours	you	this
3rd Person	they	their, theirs	them	that
Singular / Plural	who	whose	whom	the same / such

Table 21

USE OF PRONOUNS

Rule	Examples
• Make sure the reference is not ambiguous.	The foreman showed the worker how he should do it (who is "he"?).
• Use caution in referring to broad thoughts or general ideas (rather than specific nouns) with relative pronouns.	Such as "this" in the last sentence of the first paragraph under point 4.
• Consider the reader's difficulty in locating a remote antecedent.	The book was vague in the purpose of the rules of grammar and, therefore, the influence it may have had was lost.
• Watch out that "it" is not used to refer to several different antecedents or in an indefinite way.	It is not enough to be accurate, the importance of it was to be clear, rather than for it to be brief.
• I and who are used as subjects, reference to a subject, or as a subject of a noun clause, even if the total clause is used as an object.	It was _I_. John won, but <u>who</u> would have known he cheated. Harry and _I_ were cheated.
• Me and whom are used as objects, or if used as a subject of an infinitive ("to verb").	<u>Who</u> cheated <u>whom</u>? John cheated Harry and <u>me</u>.

4. PRONOUNS CAN EASILY BECOME LOST AND LOSE THE READER.

One of the more difficult problems to avoid in writing is being certain that pronouns (Table 20) are *clearly identified* with the noun (antecedent) to which they refer. This problem occurs by composing from a stream of constant thought. Pronouns are used frequently to reference the subject of a general idea which may be clearly in the front of the writer's mind, but may remain vague in the reader's mind until the entire message unfolds. This is a frequent cause of confusion.

Consider the last sentence in the above paragraph: "This is a frequent cause of confusion." The pronoun *this* refers to the entire problem of clearly identifying the antecedent of the pronoun. However, the sentence is poorly written (on purpose, to demonstrate the point) since *this* could also refer to the preceding sentence that discusses why the problem occurs. In this case, it would have been more clear to write the last sentence as follows: *"The entire problem of clearly identifying the antecedent of the pronoun is a frequent cause of confusion."*

Pronouns are unique words. They can only have meaning through association with their *antecedent*. Legal minds are carefully trained to avoid any ambiguities in this regard. Businessmen should be equally concerned; however, such ambiguities are constantly encountered. Some helpful reminders for the use of pronouns are listed in Table 21. My advice is to be sure you recognize pronouns and check your writing constantly from the reader's perspective to be sure he can only interpret the pronoun the way you intended. When in doubt, repeat the antecedent noun or resummarize the substantive thought.

Another prominent mistake relative to the use of pronouns is to use the improper case form. This is particularly true in the troublesome use of *who* or *whom*, and *I* and *me*. The rule is simply to use the subjective case (who or I) when the pronoun is used as a subject. However, in many sentences, it is difficult to define the subject or object, i.e., "Whom did you say?", where *whom* is the object of *did say*. In most situations, it is possible (and better) to avoid the use of these pronouns in business communications.

Table 22

FREQUENTLY MISUSED WORDS

Resulting From Careless Spelling

- Affect — (verb) to influence; to have an effect on
- Effect — (noun) result; (verb) to bring to pass
- Allusion — an indirect reference
- Illusion — a false impression
- Altogether — wholly
- All together — in a group
- Capital — large size letter, seat of government, financial term
- Capitol — building where government body meets
- Complement — that which completes
- Compliment — expression of praise
- Continual — occurring in steady, but not unbroken, fashion
- Continuous — without cessation
- Disinterested — to be impartial (even if interested)
- Uninterested — take no interest
- Principal — chief
- Principle — fundamental truth
- Respectfully — in a manner showing respect
- Respectively — each in the order given
- Than — used in comparisons
- Then — refers to time

Resulting From Careless Thought

- Aggravate — to add to a problem
- Irritate — to annoy
- Agree to, agree with — agree to a plan, with a person
- Alternate — every other one in a series, or a substitute
- Alternative — one of two possibilities; always a choice
- Among, between — among implies more than two; between means two
- As regards, in regard to — both correct, but not "in regards to"
- Can, may — can denotes ability, may denotes permission
- Center around, center on — has to be "on"
- Differ from, differ with — from means to be different, with means to disagree
- Good — not an adverb, used as an adjective only to mean favorable
- Well — as an adjective means "in health," as an adverb means in a good manner
- Infer — to arrive at through reasoning
- Imply — to suggest
- Regretful — sorry for
- Regrettable — unfortunate happening
- Respectfully — in a polite manner
- Respectively — each in the order given
- Should, would appreciate — should used to soften a request, would refers to anticipated action

5. MISUSAGE OF WORDS MISLEADS THE READER.

A classic advertising campaign has been developed around the comedy of Norm Crosby who purposely misuses words for a humerous, ridiculous effect. People may "extinctively ask" for Natural Beer, but I'm not sure how "appreciatory" they are. Archie Bunker is another classic in the abuse of perfectly good words that are modified to suit his purposes. Frequently, similar language is encountered at cocktail parties when the philosophizing part of the evening begins. More soberly, abuses of the language are found in every facet of life, from government publications to news articles, or from public speeches to TV and theater. It is little wonder that business writing is not immune from these transgressions.

Misusage mistakes can be grouped into two categories. The first results from *spelling errors*, either unintentional or because of ignorance, involving words that are spelled similarly but that have entirely different meanings. The second involves *incorrect usage* of a word because the writer was careless or selected a word that inaccurately represented the idea he wanted to convey. We have already discussed spelling problems, but some of the more prevalent errors that result in good words, but words that may have a different meaning than intended, are shown in Table 22. The second category (as demonstrated in Table 22 also) presents a more difficult problem for the writer to correct.

Another difficult problem in the usage of words is the use of *colloquial* or *slang* words, such as I *calculate,* for I *think*; I am *partial to,* for I *prefer;* the *thrust* of; to *fix*, for to *arrange* or *prepare; swell* and terrific. In business, it is best to avoid such phrases both from the standpoint of clarity and from the standpoint of the image they present of the author.

The only defense against misusage is to build a good vocabulary through constant attention to improving this asset. Develop a questioning habit, become well read with a critical eye, and do not hesitate to use a dictionary or thesaurus as frequently as necessary.

Table 23

THREE COMMON ERRORS OF OMISSION

1. Sentence fragments
    a.) Use of a phrase (no verb) as a sentence
       Phrase: Planning thus to eliminate confusion.
       Sentence: Such planning would thus eliminate confusion.

    b.) Use of a subordinate clause as a sentence
       Clause: Because such planning would eliminate confusion.
       Sentence: Such planning would eliminate confusion.

2. Incomplete comparisons
    a.) Use of "than" without a clear comparison
       Wrong: It appeared more like a star than a light.
       Right: It appeared more like a star than like a light.

    b.) Use of a comparison without a connector
       Wrong: This section is more difficult than spelling.
       Right: This section is more difficult than that on spelling.

3. Omission of articles, pronouns, or relative pronouns that are necessary
    a.) Articles
       We hired a carpenter and plumber (could be one person).
       We hired a carpenter and a plumber (clearly two people).

    b.) Pronouns
       Harry's wife and lover were present.
       Harry's wife and his lover were both present.

    c.) Relative pronouns
       He claimed the player who fouled caused the fumble.
       He claimed that the player who fouled caused the fumble.

---

6. LEAVING OUT NECESSARY WORDS LEAVES THE READER WONDERING.

A later chapter suggests that it is in the best interest of effective writing to write efficiently. However, some writers are brief to a fault — literally. Many words are simply necessary for finishing a thought, for good grammatical form, or for proper sentence structure. When such words are omitted, they actually reduce effectiveness. It is not unusual to find omissions in literature of highly regarded authors; however, such authors are given the benefit of any doubt, and such structure is regarded as part of their style. Advertising copy is also notorious for fragmented thoughts, and any ambiguities are excused as being clever or intentional. But average writers, particularly in normal business correspondence, usually make omissions carelessly, rather than intentionally.

Three general *omission* mistakes appear to occur frequently (Table 23). The first results in *sentence fragments*, either by omitting a verb, thus creating a phrase; or more commonly, misusing a subordinate conjunctive (*although, because, if*) or relative pronoun (*that, which, whatever*) to introduce a thought, thus creating a subordinate clause, rather than a sentence (main clause). The second category of omissions, which is particularly disruptive in achieving clear, effective communication, results in *incomplete comparisons*. Always check any sentence where "than" appears to be sure no essential words are missing. The third omission mistake is leaving out those troublesome articles (remember my former boss) and other necessary words that when missing confuse the reader. Leaving out necessary relative pronouns (particularly "that") which tend to be frequently used in business correspondence, is a prevalent mistake.

In many cases, the clarity of the thought is not reduced by an intentional omission. To continually repeat an obvious comparison, for instance, may result in an awkward flow of the main thought. A thin line exists between being too wordy or too brief. When in doubt, add the necessary words to be grammatically correct. You can never be harshly criticized for following the fundamentals.

7. SPLIT INFINITIVES SPLIT THE READER'S ATTENTION.

One of the older axioms of good grammar is never to split an infinitive, i.e., "to *carefully* write." In this example, any learned person would place carefully after write. I have never heard or seen an explanation for this that fully satisfies me. The best explanation seems to be a matter of emphasis. If you desire to give emphasis to *carefully*, splitting the infinitive achieves that end. Nevertheless, unless the split involves an extended adverbial phrase, I tend to discount the importance of this rule. Perhaps it is sufficient to rely on the advice frequently referred to in this book of sticking to the *fundamentals* whenever a choice must be made. At least you will never be considered ignorant of good grammar if you avoid splitting your infinitives.

8. DANGLING MODIFIERS RESULT IN THE READER DANGLING.

Modifiers are any words, phrases or clauses that place a restrictive meaning on the subject or substantive thought. Let's take another look at the example used in Chapter 1 to introduce you to my English teacher-turned-engineer boss.

Dangling:
Having taken the measurements, the results are obvious.

The participle phrase "Having . . ." attempts to modify results. However, this introduces an illogical or *dangling* thought, since results cannot take measurements. The correction would be:

Having taken the measurements, *I deduced the obvious results.*

Dangling modifiers are particularly ubiquitous in business writing because of the frequent need to qualify statements with restrictive modifiers. Many more examples could be cited to emphasize how easy it is to fall into a dangling trap. It should be sufficient to raise a yellow "caution" flag to be on guard for this fundamental problem. The interested reader should explore dangling modifiers in a good grammar book until a clear grasp of the principle is attained.

9. PARALLEL THOUGHTS ARE CONVEYED THROUGH PARALLEL STRUCTURE.

The concept of *parallelism* is a good fundamental to understand in order to improve the effectiveness of written communications. The term *parallel* refers simply to the form or structure of a piece of writing. It does not mean an expression of the *same* thought in a variety of ways, but rather different thoughts whose interrelationship is best expressed with a parallel format. Some examples are useful to clarify this concept:

- The objectives should assure *that* consistency is maintained, *that* system improvements are achieved, and *that* early feedback is obtained.

- The program should offer *maximum* image value, *maximum* market coverage and *maximum* profit potential.

- The objectives of such a strategy are:
  — to maximize volume,
  — to improve profitability,
  — to achieve high quality, and
  — to match competition.

Each example involves a *series* of thoughts that are related. Conceptually, parallelism embraces the simplest list to a series of complex paragraphs. The reader is able to relate easily to the intended interconnection if the writer uses consistent grammatical construction. The rule to remember is that the first element in the series establishes the format for the remainder of the items. If the first noun is preceded by an article or preposition, each noun in the series should be treated in the same manner. Likewise, if the first dot point in a list following a colon is constructed with a complete sentence, every point in the list should be a sentence. In a series of paragraphs, the first sentence should follow a consistent form to convey a continuing relationship. Attention to the fundamental concept of using parallel construction to control the reader's attention would greatly improve the effectiveness of the average writer.

SIMPLE MINDED MISTAKES

1. SPELLING MISTAKES MISTAKENLY DISTRACT THE READER.

2. IMPROPER PUNCTUATION IMPROPERLY CREATES READER CONFUSION.

3. INCONSISTENT INFLECTIONS REQUIRE READER REFLECTIONS.

4. PRONOUNS CAN EASILY BECOME LOST AND LOSE THE READER.

5. MISUAGE OF WORDS MISLEADS THE READER.

6. LEAVING OUT NECESSARY WORDS LEAVES THE READER WONDERING.

7. SPLIT INFINITIVES SPLIT THE READERS ATTENTION.

8. DANGLING MODIFIERS RESULT IN THE READER DANGLING.

9. PARALLEL THOUGHTS ARE CONVEYED THROUGH PARALLEL STRUCTURE.

By now it is clear that the simple minded mistakes outlined in this chapter, while simple to understand, are difficult to
avoid. The businessman that is interested in perfecting his writing, however, should take the time to check his composition for
such mistakes before he is finished. In particular, spelling and
punctuation mistakes can be easily found merely by rereading
the communication. I suggest rereading everything twice — the
first time for content, flow of argument, logic, and other factors
that will be covered in subsequent chapters of this book; the
second time it should be reread *slowly* to check for spelling,
punctuation and other grammatical mistakes.

Several of the other common mistakes, such as inconsistent inflections, misuse of words, errors of omission, or mishan-
dling pronouns are more a matter of practice. In the press of
business, it is especially difficult to find such errors once they
have been made. Dangling modifiers are particularly subversive
and a conscious effort must be made to root them out. It is good to
pause *while writing* whenever a modifier is added to the sentence
to be sure it is clearly related to the main clause.

The objectives of effective business writing, which are the
subjects for the remainder of this book, are achieved through
following the fundamentals. The foregoing review of such fundamentals will serve the reader well who is interested in improving
his effectiveness in written communications. All it takes is an
effort. But then, competing for promotions requires a little added
effort in every aspect of a career to achieve success.

SECTION TWO

OBJECTIVES TO IMPROVE

ORGANIZATION

3

FOR EFFECTIVE WRITING

FOCUS THE CONTENT

THE PREMISE of this book is that effective writing is dependent on understanding the objectives of a written communication. Two words in this premise are ambiguous — effective and objectives. *Effective* could either relate to accomplishing the *business* intentions of the correspondence, or to accomplishing the *writing* task of clearly enunciating and communicating your thoughts in writing to another. This book places the emphasis on the latter, with the certain knowledge that, while the business intentions may or may not be achieved based on the merits of the case presented, achieving the underlying business goals will be greatly facilitated by effectively presenting the case. *Objectives* also could refer either to the business matters being discussed, or refer specifically to the organization and approach used to write effectively. Again, defining, understanding and using sound *writing objectives*, as discussed in this book, should materially advance the achievement of the *business objectives*, as surely as they would advance the reader's clear understanding of any piece of writing, whether undertaken for business or pleasure.

The first writing objective, that of following the fundamentals, serves as the foundation for the eight other basic writing objectives in this book that all relate to improving the organization and persuasive presentation of ideas (Table 24).

Table 24

OBJECTIVES FOR EFFECTIVE WRITING
Follow the Fundamentals

Organization	Persuasiveness
• Focus the Content	• Be Absolutely Clear
• Plan the Format	• Emphasis Strategically
• Orchestrate the Logic	• Select an Appropriate Tone
	• Tailor your Style
	• Write Efficiently

Table 24

OBJECTIVES FOR EFFECTIVE WRITING
Follow the Fundamentals

Organization
- Focus the Content
- Plan the Format
- Orchestrate the Logic

Persuasiveness
- Be Absolutely Clear
- Emphasis Strategically
- Select an Appropriate Tone
- Tailor your Style
- Write Efficiently

Table 25

PRINCIPLES TO FOCUS THE CONTENT

- Prepare an outline

- Consider the audience

  — Background

  — Organizational level

  — Attitude

- Determine the essential scope
  of the subject

- Plan the necessary depth of
  coverage

- Focus strategically

Maximum effectiveness can only be achieved through careful advance planning of the *organization* of the composition. Virtually all advisors on the art of writing recommend an outline of one kind or another be prepared before composing the first sentence. This is sound advice. The outline should include the specific content to be covered in the communication, the best format for the situation at hand, and the logic or flow of argument to be utilized. Such outlines can take many forms. They may be rather formal and extensive, or they may be hastily prepared notes on the back of an envelope. The time available and complexity of the subject will usually dictate the nature of the outline, but the importance of the procedure should not be dismissed. Collecting numerous fleeting thoughts related to a topic requires concentration and effort. Usually hundreds of ideas dance around the writer's mind as a project is undertaken. Capturing central points in an organized way by making an outline will give direction and order to the composition and avoid rambling, disjointed discussion. Then too, picturing the total composition by looking at a total outline in abbreviated form frequently leads to discovering added thoughts, to including secondary points, to obtaining additional information, or to otherwise completing the picture.

Persuasiveness is the fickle element that separates truly effective writing from material that conveys information without convincing the reader to accept the material. Good organization, of course, can contribute to persuasive writing; however, other objectives will be discussed that more directly influence the reader's acceptance of the ideas presented. Acceptance does not necessarily mean endorsement of another's point of view, but it does mean recognition and understanding of the writer's ideas. This is important in establishing effectiveness regardless of whether the paper is intended merely to transmit information or to present an argument.

This chapter will discuss the need to *focus the content* of any piece of writing as the first step toward proper organization to increase effectiveness. Principles to consider to achieve better focus of the content are shown in Table 25. It is seldom necessary or advisable for the writer to communicate everything he knows about a subject. The purpose should be to clearly communicate thoughts, not to impress the reader of the brilliance of the writer. When the reader must search through pages of writing to cull out the important information, the temptation is always great to shortcut the process. In many cases, readers take the optimum shortcut; they simply throw the document away. Left to his own devices, the reader may select content that the writer had no intention of emphasizing or miss the intended major points. In any case, the writer gains little credit for superfluous content and runs a high risk of spoiling the effectiveness of the entire effort if he succumbs to the temptation of overwriting.

CONSIDER THE AUDIENCE

The initial requirement in achieving proper focus is to *consider the audience*. Most communications result from some background circumstances. The paper may be a letter in reply to a previous letter or verbal request. It may be the latest of a continuing series of papers on a subject, such as a status report. It could be a recommendation to initiate action on the reader's part resulting from mutual business interactions. It could also be merely an informative document conveying budgets, market conditions, competitive actions, or other material. In any situation, the writer should consider the reader's knowledge, or lack of knowledge, of the background circumstances in order to determine the appropriate content.

The reader's previous exposure or advance knowledge of the subject being written about should dictate the general *scope* and *depth of coverage* required to effectively communicate the principle ideas. However, in a business environment, numerous individuals frequently may receive the paper. It is possible, and even usual, that many of the recipients will have different levels of background knowledge. An engineer writing to a marketing manager may include the controllers office, manufacturing management, and other engineering organizations on the distribution list. The needs of all parties must be taken into account. If the primary intent is to discuss a marketing matter, less extensive technical information may be appropriate. However, many ways exist to expand the content for all concerned, such as references to related reports, inclusion of contacts to be used for additional information, or adding appendices to the primary paper.

The organizational level of the audience is another fundamental consideration. A general rule of thumb is that the higher the level of the audience, the broader the scope of content and the shallower the depth of material required for effective communication. This is over simplified, of course, and could easily backfire unless the writer has a thorough understanding of the requirements of his audience. One clear indication of ineffectiveness is a rapid reply from the reader requesting additional information — a device prominently used by many at the slightest provocation as a means to defer, delay, or otherwise avoid action.

It is no accident that a consistent characteristic of above average performers in a company is the ability to project their thoughts to be comparable to those of managers above them — to anticipate how higher management would be thinking and the requirements they would have for information on any subject. The discipline of consciously considering the approach of focusing the content of any communication will improve any writer's ability to elevate their thinking to accomplish this end.

Considering the needs of the audience is equally important for correspondence that flows down the ladder as well as up (or across). Effectiveness of these communications can also be greatly improved by the proper concern for focusing the content and anticipating the requirements of the recipients down the ladder. The total amount of lost productivity nationwide due to ineffectiveness and wasted effort resulting from poor communications down the ladder staggers the imagination. Attention to the concept of recognizing the background information of the readers and focusing the content to the needs of the primary audience, would lead to more thoughtful communications from the top down, which would greatly improve operating efficiency. This is valid whether the communication is an informal buck slip, the initiation of a broad assignment, or a formal policy statement.

DETERMINE THE SCOPE

Focusing the content requires planning the scope of coverage. The circumstances that initiated the letter or paper, as well as the primary audience, will usually dictate the scope. However, care must be taken to limit the scope to essential material. It is particularly damaging to effectiveness to digress into irrelevant matters. For instance, if a letter is being written about the reliability of a design modification to a carburetor, it could be distracting to offer, "Although the design has not been costed, we anticipate a modest piece cost penalty." The cost may be irrelevant to the reliability discussion. On the other hand, if the intent is to recommend *approval* of the design change, the scope would probably have to include a full financial discussion, supply or manufacturing issues, timing considerations, and other matters.

Scope is certainly a matter of judgment on the part of the writer and the most effective writers will exercise good judgment in directing the focus of the content.

PLAN THE DEPTH OF COVERAGE

In the same manner, the depth of coverage of the material presented is a critical consideration. It might have been necessary in the above example to explain that testing was satisfactorily completed on the redesigned carburetor. If the primary audience for the letter was engineering management, it may also have been necessary to include information on the specific testing program, e.g., the number of samples, statistical information on cycles tested, number of failures, mode of failure, environmental conditions, and testing parameters. A member of senior management, on the other hand, may find such detail distracting (if he was able to interpret it at all) and would probably rather know simply that his engineering managers had verified the reliability of the design with adequate testing. Again, the writer must exercise good judgment in focusing the content to the needs of the audience when selecting the depth of detail discussed on a subject.

One aspect of depth of coverage frequently encountered is the desire to amplify points being made by citing supporting examples or antidotes. While useful and sometimes necessary to take this approach, the inexperienced writer may have difficulty in knowing when to stop. Usually, it should require no more than two examples, and preferably only one, to fully clarify an ambiguous point. The more examples used, the more likely they may not all apply precisely to the point, which may undermine clarity. Likewise, *antidotes* should be used sparingly. In normal business communications, antidotes seem out of place and are seldom used. To relate that a situation was "like the traveling salesman that . . .," or "similar to the time the retiring football player said . . .," is basically not conducive to serious acceptance of the point being made. If it is believed that an antidote is necessary for clarification, or even to pump some life into a dreary discourse, it is better to use business antidotes. The frequency of use of examples in a discussion should be limited to those necessary for clear understanding of the communication, nothing more.

FOCUS STRATEGICALLY

Compositions that involve presenting an argument require separate considerations relative to the focus of the content. The writer should always have a position to take and the focus must be tailored accordingly. Few things are more damaging to a career than indecisiveness or timidity in drawing a conclusion.

Arguments, no matter how thoroughly presented, will always be less effective unless the writer has a *clear point of view* in mind. The reader may disagree with the conclusion, but it is necessary for full understanding for him to know where the writer stands. To present arguments without advocating a position dilutes the relative significance of the points and may lead to improper conclusions. Furthermore, managers abhor being placed in the position of "here are all the facts, now you decide (that's what you get paid for.)"

The writer's point of view should determine the focus of the content when presenting an argument. Effectiveness is enhanced by looking at both sides of the argument, but the writer should emphasize the content that supports his conclusion. When planning such a paper, it is important to fully develop the alternative arguments and consider every possible negative, as well as the positive, arguments. However, as will be discussed in more detail in the chapter on logic, when advocating a position, it is unnecessary to over-emphasize the opponents arguments; to do so is undermining to the effectiveness of the paper. The focus of the discussion of the opponent's views should be to refute such arguments with convincing counterpoints or by comparison with the greater importance of positive points.

Focusing the argument requires an open-minded, questioning attitude toward the subject. The writer must clearly identify his thesis, i.e., the major point or points that he will attempt to persuade the reader to accept. Then the self-questioning should begin in earnest. What are the possible opposing points of view? What are the relationships between the writer's positive arguments and the opposing views? What are the limitations or qualifications on either side? Are all the points covered and are they all relevant? Finally, which arguments on either side are most persuasive (from the writer's viewpoint? from the opposite viewpoint?) and what is the clincher? If you can identify the central issue, the focus of the whole becomes clear.

Good judgment, essential in planning the scope and depth of coverage, is also necessary to avoid being overly narrow-minded in determining the focus. Many instances come to mind where it may be desirable to expand the subject matter to the advantage of the writer. For example, a request for quotation of a bid on a job may lack certain elements that could be key to winning a contract. Rather than focusing solely on the requested information, the reply to such a letter could be expanded to include other relevant information, e.g., an engineering support organization that your competitors may not have. Another example would be in cases where the writer may be responding to a proposal and has an alternative to suggest. Such an expansion of the focus is actually a hallmark of upward bound executives who exhibit an ability to add new ideas, to suggest different approaches, and to present new alternatives for consideration. Such creativity should not be stifled by a rigid concept of focus. The point is that focus should be *controlled* by the writer, and the focus should serve his intended purposes. In this context, such an expansion of the subject matter would not be a digression resulting in an ineffective communication as long as it was relevant to the issues being discussed.

The conscientious writer, interested in improving the effectiveness of his communications, should adopt the objective of improving the organization of his material through focusing the content strategically. A good mechanism to assure proper focus is to prepare an outline in advance of writing. The outline should be a working tool that remains flexible within reason. If a good idea comes to you while you are writing, which frequently happens, do not hesitate to use it, just because you did not anticipate it while preparing the outline. But check carefully at such a point for relevancy; the odds are good that if the idea was important it would have come to you initially.

The primary considerations to achieve better focus are the backgrounds and needs of the primary audience, the scope of coverage required for completeness, and the depth of coverage essential for clear understanding. Strategically focusing the content requires sound judgment to be sure the piece of writing is totally complete for the purpose at hand, without introducing irrelevant material. This judgment is a matter of experience and business accumen, but recognition of the concept of focus and the diligent practice of this writing objective will improve your skills in this area. Organizing your composition begins with carefully planning the focus in advance; and should end with a final check of the written material to test (1) whether everything that should be included has been, and (2) whether everything that was included, was necessary, relevant, and to the point. Such an approach would dramatically improve the effectiveness of many business communications.

4

FOR EFFECTIVE WRITING

PLAN THE FORMAT

THE PLANNING stage prior to writing a communication involves deciding how to focus the content, how to most effectively format the writing, and broadly how to orchestrate the logic. These steps may flash through the mind of a well trained writer in a matter of seconds as he jots notes on a pad before dictating a memo, or the process may involve hours of preparation with carefully prepared outlines; sometimes the outlines become the subject of separate meetings and discussions prior to initiating the writing. In any case, the planning stage is crucial to the success of any well written communication. The key elements of achieving focus have been discussed. Before discussing certain important concepts related to logic in the next chapter, this chapter will discuss the importance of an often overlooked aspect of creating an effective piece of writing — the *visual format* of the material. Principles for planning the format are shown in Table 26.

Table 26

PRINCIPLES FOR PLANNING THE FORMAT

- Consider the medium of the communication
- Strive for an overall positive impression
- Be neat, orderly and complete
- Control initial impressions and skimming
- Control the reader's thought process
- Utilize conventional formats
- Consider any technique that will aid comprehension

Before considering the details related to handling presently accepted formats most effectively, it is reasonable to question whether present formatting concepts may soon be archaic given the explosion in modern communication technology. The dawning age of sophisticated electronic and video communication systems will undoubtedly impact in many respects on the physical form of written communications.

A massive effort is underway, in fact, to make obsolete the standard, neatly typed, 8½" x 11" business letter. This method of communicating ideas and retaining information consumes an enormous amount of productive manpower; even considering the modern self-correcting, high-speed typewriters, dictating equipment and supporting equipment — all designed to facilitate the transposition of ideas floating around in the writer's mind onto a piece of paper that can be read by another to obtain those ideas.

Much has been written about the sheer burden of storing such documents, as well as storing the material for preparing the paper in the first place, including enough material-on-hand to support several rough drafts, corrected pages, and false starts. The typical office is literally being buried in paperwork. Thousands are involved in the maintenance of this system; from the managers, to the secretaries, to the file clerks, to the mail room, to the trash disposal personnel. Nevertheless, very few companies have made progress toward reducing the amount of communication that is transmitted in writing from one to another.

Predictably, the written form of communication will remain an important element of business transactions for the lifetime of those inclined to read this book; therefore, the nature of the physical result of such communications, the *format* of such documents, if you will, should remain a matter of interest. The technology exists to implement the totally integrated communication systems envisioned by the office management planners of the future — computerized information storage and retrieval systems, telecommunications with amazing capabilities to combine the impact of visual, oral and printed media, voice driven machines that would virtually eliminate secretaries (God forbid!), and remote terminal devices that even avoid the need for people to have close proximity to one another as they conduct business.

Such systems are fascinating to contemplate, and as a businessman I have a keen appreciation for the importance they will undoubtedly have for improving the efficiency of communications. To continue to progress as a nation, with the need for transmitting, digesting and utilizing information growing in geometric proportions, such systems will be mandatory. However, implementing such a massive transition of the hundreds of thousands of business offices of all types and sizes to the Twenty First Century communications systems will entail an incalculable number of written letters, reports, contracts, etc. of the present format for many decades.

Before dropping this matter of the possible technological obsolescence of communicating in written form, which I believe is important for every student or practitioner of business to appreciate and adapt to, it is useful to consider certain fundamentals of communications that will remain, regardless of the technology utilized. In the first place, person-to-person communications are at the core of human existence. No matter how intelligent we make machines, interpersonal exchanges of ideas will never be totally replaced by machine-to-machine technology. Therefore, the essential requirements for effective communications between people should hold true regardless of the media used. For example, the objective of carefully planning ahead to focus the content of a message and to organize the material in a logical manner would seem sensible in any environment.

The concept of formatting the message strategically to improve effectiveness will also remain a valid objective; however, the formats of the future may not resemble present accepted practices. Even if the words are displayed on a video screen, rather than the standard 8½" x 11" paper, it will be necessary for an individual to determine the specific appearance of the message to be shown to the viewer. To the extent that one format achieves the objectives of effective communications — clarity, emphasis, simplicity, etc.— and another format fails, the underlying goals of the one initiating the message will be best met by considering the most effective format.

WHAT IS *FORMAT*?

The format of a written communication refers to its visual appearance. The appearance of a letter or report plays a vital role in achieving effectiveness. It may help or hinder achieving full understanding of the message with the minimum effort and the minimum confusion on the reader's part. It also creates a signific-ant first impression that conveys information about the writer to the reader, over and above the words on the page. A messy letter with smudge marks, typos or typeovers, lines running off at a slanted angle, erratic margins and a signature squeezed into the bottom right hand corner, would be a poor introduction for any business transaction. The rationalization that a lack of time, due to the rush of business, prevents correction of sloppy work is a shortsighted argument. The writer should never underestimate the importance of the visual appearance of his work.

Although many books contain instructions on the "proper" format for business letters, essays or reports, experience clearly demonstrates that no single form is always "best." Rather the format should be planned for the communication task at hand. Admittedly, some basic essentials can be discussed, as will be covered in this chapter, but if a student of business attempts to duplicate the prescribed formats found in many writing manuals for actual business situations, he may be unwittingly limiting the effectiveness of his writing. It was tempting, when preparing this book, to include a standard section on appropriate formats for business letters, e.g., the proper heading content and spacing, margins, accepted ways to paragraph, the salutation, etc. This book will leave that to others and treat these matters in the general context of controlling the format, rather than the format controlling the writing. It is important for the neophite writer to recognize that certain formats are accepted, to learn them in the beginning, and to be aware when he is deviating from the norm. As he progresses in his writing skills, he must learn to control the format to his advantage if he is to achieve maximum effective-ness.

INITIAL IMPRESSIONS AND SKIMMING

The first thing to recognize is the importance of the initial impression the reader will form upon seeing the communication. This first visual impression can work to the benefit of the writer, or against him, but is seldom neutral. The impression results from the overall format or the total appearance of the communi-cation. Consider for a moment how a typical person may actually read a letter. Upon receiving a letter, I follow a routine before I begin reading:

- I glance at the envelope and notice the company logo, return address, and whether it was addressed to me personally or my organization. (I may even glance at the stamp, which sometimes conveys more about the author than he wants for me to know.)
- Taking out the letter, I quickly glance at the type of communication it is — a quick one-pager, a thick report with multi-tabbed appendices, a routine weekly report on sales, a trade publication, a letter with pictures or samples attached, or whatever.
- In a matter of seconds, I take in the date, the addressees and carbon copy recipients (who else is involved), and flip back to see who signed the thing — if I don't know him, I look again for identification of the writer; title, address or whatever.
- Next I look for the subject — if it's a report, the title of the work; if a letter, hopefully the writer has been kind enough to include a "subject" line; if not, I start glancing around until I find the subject. A typical businessman deals with numerous subjects every day and it is necessary to get oriented as each new piece of paper is picked up from the In-Box.
- I have to admit, I usually then cheat and skip to the ending, reading that first. I like to see what the writer wants — his recommendations, conclusions or requests. This may be inconsistent with the common advice to concentrate on the introduction when preparing a written communication; I suppose many people do read the introduction first, although I predict that many skip to the ending next. Either way, the reader's inclination is to quickly find out the purpose of the document and what is expected of him as a result.
- Finally, I will sit back and read the document as extensively as necessary (notice I did not say completely) to satisfy my requirements.

If my habits are typical, it is readily apparent how much "work" a good format has accomplished for the writer before I start slugging through his carefully constructed composition. An inexperienced writer could greatly improve the effectiveness of his work by simply visualizing what the recipient is likely to do with it. Formatting techniques have two basic objectives:

(1) to control the reader's thought process, and

(2) to facilitate the reader's rapid, accurate under-standing of the material.

Control is achieved in several ways. As mentioned, the reader's initial impression of the writer is formed from the overall appearance of the transmittal. A positive impression puts the reader in a receptive frame of mind, regardless of the contents. A negative impression distracts the reader and impairs effective communication — thoughts such as, Why did he use such small stationery? Can you imaging writing a job interview request on notebook paper? Doesn't the dummy even know how to spell my name right? and many others that result from carelessness or lack of concern for appearances now have to be overcome by some brilliant writing.

Beyond controlling the reader's initial impression, a good format can also control the way a reader skims the letter initially, similar to the way I described my own habits. By planning the location and content of address blocks, headings and sub-headings, signature blocks, sub-titles, and other elements of a report or letter, the writer can catch the skimmer's attention and direct it accordingly. It is wise, for instance, to indent and underline a sub-title for "Recommendations," since it can be antici-pated the reader will search for it at any time he chooses, rather than waiting for the text to lead him up to it step-by-step as he reads the entire document. The idea is to consider how the paper will be read and to create visual methods for controlling the reader.

Control is also essential throughout the paper, after the initial impact of the format and skimming process has been ac-complished. Much of the remainder of this book will be devoted to *control* (through emphasis, logic, tone, style, etc.). With respect to the format, control is achieved through the structure of the com-position, through effective paragraphing, and through good sentence structure.

CONTROL THROUGH STRUCTURE

The fundamental structure for writing on any subject is to have:

- An introduction that conveys the main purpose of the communication and sufficient background material to orient the reader as to why the writer is communicating to him,
- The main body, which transmits information, or develops a thesis, or communicates the basic message regarding the introduction, and
- A conclusion that summarizes what has been said and conveys what the writer intends for the reader to do next, if anything.

Over and over again this simple format is demonstrated to be the most effective way to communicate ideas. First, tell the reader what you are going to say, then say it, then tell him what you said. This same structure is also utilized for effective paragraphs.

A good paragraph contains an introduction, or topic sentence, then several sentences that elaborate on the subject, and then a closing sentence. An effective format will contain well conceived paragraphs that are easy to read, easy to follow, and easy to comprehend. Such paragraphs will have the consistency of a single major point, and will avoid mixing several points within the same paragraph. This format controls the reader because, if followed faithfully throughout the letter, he knows a new paragraph is introducing a new point and he can easily shift with the writer. On the other hand, if any paragraph contains more than one point, the reader will be distrustful of all of the paragraphing, and control will be lost.

The smallest element for formatting control grammatically is the sentence. Control can be gained or lost in a variety of ways through sentence structure. Many of these have been covered in the former chapters on grammar fundamentals, and more will be included in later chapters. From a format standpoint, the basic advice is to avoid introducing unrelated thoughts in the same sentence. A new sentence should be a clear signal to the reader that the writer is about to express a new thought — he can count on it.

FORMATTING TECHNIQUES

Many techniques are available to control the reader's attention and facilitate understanding through the visual format. Spacing of margins, headings, titles, and indentations can direct the eye and give balance and organization to the paper. The use of capital letters and underlining for critical sub-titles sets them apart from the text. Occasionally it is appropriate to box-in a key statement or summary thought to give maximum emphasis to the point. In many cases, the text can be interrupted strategically to include a schedule of numerical data or other facts that will reinforce a point. Within the body of the text, quotation marks, parenthesis signs, dash or ellipses marks, indented phrases, and colons followed by dot points are all formatting methods for controlling the reader's attention and facilitating the reader's full understanding of the material.

In a business context, as many specific formats exist as there are needs for communication. The challenge for effective writing is to consider the visual effects of the communication and to utilize any technique available that will assist in clearly presenting ideas. However, an upward bound businessman will be observant and alert for certain formatting techniques that are more acceptable than others within his own business environment.

Every profession, every industry, every occupation has recurring communication needs, and those aware of the importance of the visual format will be alert for consistent, or frequently used, techniques. Stock brokers communications do not resemble those between heavy construction companies; the automotive industry has unique needs for communication from the garmet industry; government operates differently than private entrepreneurs.

The form of communication may be quite different if it is intended for use within the company or to be sent to an outside client or supplier. Within my company, communications from Finance Staff are easily identifiable by their visual appearance, as are those from the Corporate Strategy Staff, Sales Operations, or Engineering — organizations frequently adopt a formatting style to facilitate communications. Format techniques may even vary if it is a memo within the department or a note to other functional activities within the company.

Care should be taken when a writer desires to introduce a

new format for any of these recurring communication channels. It could be more effective to use established formats that the reader will readily recognize and easily follow. If a writer becomes too creative in formatting techniques, it can be counterproductive to effectiveness. But he must make a conscious decision regarding the details of the format, i.e., either to use an established format, modify it, or develop a new format, to maximize the visual impact of his work.

Although it is important to avoid rigidly following any formatting techniques, it is helpful to summarize certain standard methods that may be considered as the writer organizes the composition. General formats for common business communications are summarized in Table 27.

Table 27

BUSINESS COMMUNICATIONS FORMATS

- The Standard Business Letter
- The Memo
- The Essay
- The Report
- The "Text Book" Format
- The "Slide" Format
- The Executive Summary
- The Attachments

THE STANDARD BUSINESS LETTER

The most frequently used format is the business letter. The visual appearance of letters may vary widely but certain characteristics prevail. The format is as follows:

LETTER HEAD
Normally used by established businesses and includes the sender's company identification, dates, and other data, e.g., slogans. This block may be omitted for letters between individuals or by someone non-affiliated with a company, e.g., a job resume letter.

ADDRESSEE HEADING
Identification of the intended recipient of the letter. It may include several names, or one name with others receiving copies listed separately. In many cases, the "carbon copy" recipients are listed on the bottom of the last page of the letter. When addressed to an individual, the heading should include complete identification, including job position title and company mailing address, in addition to the individual's name.

SALUTA- TION
The use of "Dear John" is an accepted custom that is never interpreted to seriously mean an expression of affection or endearment. It is nothing more than a courtesy to acknowledge that the writer knows who he is writing to. Much has been written advising different approaches to the salutation that are considered appropriate for different situations. The writing student should familiarize himself with these customs, as well as the accepted practices in his business. One tip especially deserving mention, however, is to use the individual's full name (spelled properly) whenever possible. It is always a more effective beginning than "To whom it may concern."

SUBJECT OR INTRO- DUCTION
This block is frequently omitted and the content included in an introductory paragraph. Including a simple statement or phrase indicating the subject of the letter is helpful to orient the reader and for ease of reference in subsequent correspondence. It greatly improves effectiveness and the reader will appreciate it. Also, it is helpful to include any reference information that relates to the letter, e.g., a report, a meeting, or a previous letter.

BODY OF LETTER
The format of the content will vary as widely as the subjects covered in the millions of daily transactions. As mentioned earlier, however, it will normally include an introduction, message, and summary with any number of pages, exhibits, or attachments.

STANDARD BUSINESS LETTER (continued)

The "close" is emphasized as a separate block because of its importance to effectiveness. This is where the business purpose the writer has in mind will be fulfilled. A clearly written summary, conclusions, recommendations, or request for action may salvage accomplishing the desired results, even though other aspects of the format may be defective. Whenever possible, the *close* should clearly be identified with a separate heading.

> CLOSE

Again a common courtesy that recognizes an established tradition. It may seem superfluous to indicate the writer's sincerity, but it is harmless to use the customary form. Much advice has been published on "proper" messages for a close. It is best to use one accepted in the writer's business, or simply "Regards."

> REGARDS

In addition to the writer's full name (both signed and typed), the block gives the reader a return address and other necessary information for a response, e.g., title or phone numbers.

> WRITER
> IDENTI-
> FICATION

THE MEMO

The memo may be the most versatile and intriguing format for communicating in writing. No "standard" format for the memo can be defined and yet any businessman can recognize a memo. It can be an effective tool for making the machinery of business run smoothly, or it can be the source of tremendous inefficiency. Someday I would like to devote a separate book entirely to the use and misuse of the ubiquitous business memo.

In essence, the memo can be likened to an abbreviated business letter. It is condensed into only essential information. Since the sender usually knows the recipient and vice versa, addressees are omitted. Salutations and regards are unnecessary and either omitted or limited to first names or other informalities. Some memos are relegated to standard forms where the writer merely checks the appropriate boxes to route it properly, send a message, request action, and conduct business.

For all of its lack of specific information, the simple memo can be a very powerful communication. Winston Churchill conducted the British effort throughout his administration and during World War II almost entirely with the memo, and later wrote at length in eloquent detail about his experiences. One executive's memo to another attached to a 250 page report may simply state, "Recommendation makes sense. Let's go. See me in 5 days with results." Things will start happening. Another executive may send a memo saying, "Wonder if we should look into this?" Depending on the circumstances, his subordinate may scribble "Yes" on it and send it back, or he might establish a new task force to conduct a six month study based on the memo. Few memos are ignored, but unless they are thoughtfully written, the intent of the writer of the memo may or may not be fulfilled.

THE ESSAY

The essay is a form of writing that is painfully familiar to all Freshmen English composition students, but seldom encountered in its *pure* form in a business environment. An essay is a piece of writing to express the author's opinion about a subject with a supporting argument in defense of such an opinion. Volumes have been written on writing effective essays, from simple one page compositions to the ultimate collegiate challenge, the term paper. Distilled down, certain consistent parameters set apart the essay form from other communications. An essay is always a presentation of an argument in support of an opinion. A discourse transmitting factual information is a report, not an essay. A letter requesting information is a letter, not an essay. A memo is not an essay.

The importance of the essay form is to understand the format, or structure, that most educators advise to be the most effective for convincing the reader of the merits of the writer's opinion. Many business situations require the presentation of an argument, resulting in a recommended course of action, which is no more than the writer's opinion about what should be done. Therefore, you find the essay form at work in many business communications, possibly as part of a report, as part of a letter, or as a separate communication. A major business paper frequently has more than one essay, e.g., the paper on the long range operating plans for a corporate business strategy. As in any argument, the structure is the familiar one: introduce the subject, present both sides of the argument, and draw valid conclusions. The general format of an essay is, therefore, as follows:

INTRO-DUCE THE THESIS	The thesis is a clear statement of the author's opinion on a single, argumentative aspect of a subject. The key words are *opinion* and *argumentative*. Without these characteristics, the topic is not an essay. The introduction must clarify for the reader the author's exact opinion and explain the fundamental thesis. It must transmit the central point, i.e., "define the thesis."
PRESENT THE ARGUMENT • Negative view • Rebuttal • Positive view	The main body of the essay format is devoted to presenting the argument in support of the author's thesis. Without dwelling on this gigantic subject, suffice it to say that the argument should present both points of view to be most convincing. The underlying logic will be discussed in more detail in the next chapter. The format may be simple or very elaborate, running hundreds of pages, with supporting data, exhibits and appendices.
SUMMARY AND CONCLU-SIONS	Using the weight of the various arguments presented in the body of the essay, the author summarizes the critical points that have led him to develop the opinion he holds. The techniques used to accomplish this most effectively are the subject of some debate. As a pragmatic businessman, in the final analysis, the "facts" (true or imputed), honestly presented, should be sufficient to win support — assuming the author has adequate business accumen and judgment to form a sound opinion.

THE REPORT

The next general format for business communications is the report — a broad umbrella, encompassing any communication of factual information. When the report concludes with recommended actions, it can be considered a variation of the essay form, since by definition, the recommendations are supported (or not) by the body of the report, hence it forms the argument. The best example of a report format is the annual report issued by corporations to their stockholders. However, literally thousands of formats for reports exist in business — from the expense account report, to the status report on project progress, to the office workplan for the next quarter, to the manufacturing inventory control report. Each has a unique formatting requirement, but the visual appearance of the report can materially assist in effectively communicating the information by

TEXT BOOK FORMAT

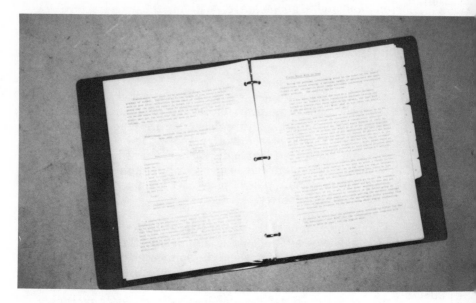

SLIDE FORMAT

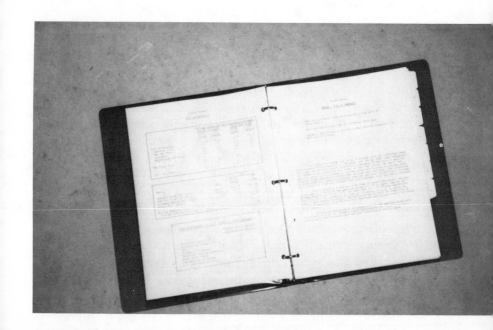

controlling the thought process, and by facilitating the rapid, accurate understanding of the material.

GENERAL PRESENTATION FORMATS

Within the general formats of an essay or report, several concepts related to presentation formats may be of interest to the novice businessman. Broadly, two writing presentation techniques dominate — the first, I refer to as the *text book* format, the second, as the *slide* format (because it lends itself to presenting slides on a screen for an oral presentation). Other general presentation format considerations involve the use of "Executive Summaries," attached exhibits, and appendices. Each of these formats will be mentioned in this chapter to complete the summary of normal formats encountered in business writing.

THE TEXT BOOK FORMAT

As its name implies, this format is similar to that found in many text books — the text is organized into various "chapters" (more normally in business papers identified simply with subtitles) setting apart discussion on a single topic or related subjects. The discussion frequently is interrupted with supporting statistical data, summary lists, or even pictures; this is accomplished with or without reference to supporting exhibits found at the end of the paper. The objective is for the text to be self-supporting, and therefore, the information is sufficiently inclusive to obviate the need to refer to attached exhibits, except for subsequent review.

THE SLIDE FORMAT

The *slide* format is substantially different from the text book approach. It consists of a facing page of supporting data organized as though it were to be shown on a screen in the conference room. The text page is designed to elaborate on the "slide" to make the desired points. Each page (left and right facing pages) is a self-contained subject.

Both formats, the text book and the slide, have advantages and disadvantages, and either can be effective depending on the circumstances. The choice is one of *control*. If it is important to dwell on a point in order to achieve full understanding before moving on, the slide format may offer the best control, since the reader cannot skip ahead to the next subject without turning the page. On the other hand, continuity throughout the paper may be easier to achieve with a text book format. The slide format can be useful where the supporting statistics are of primary importance, since it can be distracting to interrupt the flow of a text book with a full page of data, or alternatively, flip back and forth between the text and exhibits attached at the back of the paper. The primary objective in selecting one format versus the other is to establish control.

EXECUTIVE SUMMARY

The executive summary is a formatting device frequently used in business in situations where a communication is intended for use by several levels of management, or it is desirable to have an abbreviated form of a comprehensive paper for other reasons. For example, a meeting to discuss a major paper may limit the discussion to the text of an executive summary, and a more comprehensive discussion paper may be filed with the meeting secretary for the record. In other cases, it may be convenient for senior management to read an abbreviated version, saving the full report for review when time allows, or not at all.

Executive summaries are probably the most demanding communication encountered by business writers. To be effective, they must be the epitome of the concepts described in this book. Clarity, brevity, and comprehensive organization are required. The focus, the format, and the logic must be impeccible. The format is succient, and yet complete. The structure, however, follows the form of the supporting paper and always includes a purpose, or introduction, the essence of the body of the paper, and a summary conclusion or recommendation.

CONSIDER THE ATTACHMENTS

Many otherwise effective business communication formats have been ruined through lack of consideration of the attached material — the objective and visual requirements of the attachments are just as fundamental to effective communication as the body of the paper. The actual format of the attachments (organization, headings, etc.), of course, can lead to rapid, clear comprehension, or add to the confusion. Attached exhibits and appendices should be carefully (and strategically) referenced in the body of the paper, with maximum consideration given to control of the reader's use of such material. For example, it may be critical to locate the reference to an attachment at the end of a paragraph to better control comprehension of a thought, rather than inserting it in the middle of a paragraph or sentence.

As another example, a statistic cited in the text may be derived from subtracting two numbers shown separately on an attached schedule — how much more effective it is to show the derived number on the attachment and even circling it, for easy access. Examples of appropriate uses and abuses of attachments are too numerous to mention; however, the fundamental is important — the visual impact of the use of attached data has a basic role to play in achieving effectiveness of the entire format of the paper.

This chapter offers a brief summary of the importance of planning the most effective format to present ideas in writing. This concept is no more than a recognition of the fact that understanding is passed from one to another through use of the sences (sight, hearing, touch, taste, and smelling), and the only one of importance to a writer is vision. Everything achieved in writing is a function of the visual interpretation of the printed matter on the page. In another era, it may be transmitted by viewing such matter on a video-screen or other device, but this fundamental form of communication, obtaining another's thoughts through a visual interpretation of symbols, will remain. The format of this information can be conducive to controlling the reader's thought process and facilitating understanding, or it can defeat this process. Those aspiring to write their way up the ladder would do well to keep sight of this fundamental concept, integrate it into their preparation when writing, observe the customs and conventions of their business, particularly those of people considered to be successful, and perfect the art of effectively formatting their written work.

5

FOR EFFECTIVE WRITING

ORCHESTRATE THE LOGIC

THE THIRD area of organization for effective writing that requires advance preparation and planning is to orchestrate the logic. Principles to be discussed in this chapter are shown in Table 28.

Table 28

PRINCIPLES FOR ORCHASTRATING THE LOGIC

- Plan the logic in advance
- Group common thoughts or data
- Present the writer's point of view
- "Funnel" down or "Pyramid" up
- Utilize the accepted psychology of argument
- Control the logic with fundamental techniques

As we have seen, two general forms of communication exist in any business environment; the first *transmits information* only, without leading to a conclusion or recommendation; the second presents an *argument*, or at least builds a case for some conclusion or recommended action. Some communications may serve both functions, of course. The logic utilized in presenting the material for either of the two communications is considerably different, although some similarities exist.

It would be enlightening for those outside of business to witness the widespread lack of attention to rudimentary forms of logical organization of thoughts in business communications. On the other hand, such carelessness appears to exist in many government writings as well, and may also be prevalent in religious or educational institutions, and other fields outside the business sector.

I am not referring to sophisticated forms of logic as practiced in courtroom trials or in writing Supreme Court decisions, but rather to basic, simple, common sense ideas of order and consistency that lead to coherent thoughts and overall control. The intent of this book is not to educate the reader on the philosophy or principles of logic, the use of empirical versus implicative evidence, nor the difference between deductive and inductive reasoning. I will humbly limit myself to less scholarly, but hopefully more practical, discussion.

It is amazing how frequently the average businessman encounters disorganized, illogical and confusing communications. The remedy is simple. *Take the time* when planning and outlining a composition to orchestrate the logic, so the reader can follow the tune without missing a beat.

This chapter will attempt to provide helpful, general concepts to improve the logic in frequently encountered business communications. While it is difficult to cover the wide variety and demands for all types of business communications in a brief, general discussion, the concepts should be applicable to most situations. The writing objective to keep in mind, however, is to *plan* the logical flow of your writing; incorporate this objective into the way you think.

Make *logical organization* an integral part of developing sentences, paragraphs, and the total work. Test your outline against this standard before you start, and consider it again as you reread the final letter or paper. You will see a substantial improvement in the effectiveness of your writing if you will only take the time to root out illogical or poorly organized thoughts. It's an effort that may get you moving, and keep you moving, up the ladder.

LOGICAL ORGANIZATION

It is hard to conceive of a subject that does not lend itself to some degree of organization. Even the communications that are intended only to transmit information can be organized to facilitate understanding. Their structure may be less definitive than one presenting an orderly argument, but some logical concepts can be described. We have discussed previously the benefits of properly introducing any subject — the reinforcement effect of a format that tells the reader what will be said, then to say it, then to summarize what has been said. An introduction to an expository letter or paper should clarify the intent of the communication, the limits or focus of the content, and give a clue as to the organization of the material. The structure of the body of the communication should also convey to the reader the intended order or logic of the presentation of the material.

One organizational principle for the structure is simply the idea of grouping common thoughts or data. Normally, any subject lends itself to some grouping of logical sub-topics. One company's annual report may group the discussion by product line, another's by organizational component (sales, manufacturing, divisions, etc.), but some order will be evident. In the same manner, a sales report, or engineering project status report, or letter transmitting a quotation can be grouped logically. The grouping, if readily apparent to the reader, facilitates rapid comprehension and controls the train of thought of the reader — just what the writer wants. A random collection of thoughts may cover the subject, but effectiveness will be greatly improved by a logical grouping of the material.

When grouping, it is necessary to pick some common thread running through the material. In some cases the grouping may be obvious, in others it may require careful thought. The choice is one of emphasis, which will be discussed later, but the concept is to consider the intent of the writer *to organize the reader's thoughts* and group the content to control that process.

For example, a report could be organized chronologically or by subject (financial, marketing, product line, etc.). The writer should consider whether it is more important to the reader to think primarily of the chronology, or more important to concentrate on one subject at a time. In another case, the grouping may be in rank order of importance, i.e., from most profitable to least profitable, largest to smallest, highest cost to least cost, or smallest volume to largest volume.

Many marketing discussions lend themselves to grouping by market segmentation or different consumer groups. Engineering discussions could be organized by product line or testing program. A manufacturing review could be grouped by plant, or by organization cutting across several plants (salaried and hourly workforce, or plant engineering and maintenance, etc.). The consistent considerations are that the common thread have some logical basis, that the grouping once selected be carefully followed throughout the paper so the reader will "trust" it, and lastly that the grouping imparts the intended emphasis desired by the writer.

Another concept that could be useful when writing either to transmit information or to present an argument is the simple notion of *funneling down*. The organization in this case is to begin with a broad subject and funnel down to secondary divisions of the subject, to finally focus on a specific detail of the subject. An example might be a discussion of a decline in national sales of a product, then a review of regional performance, with a final focus on the most critical collapse in key states or cities. In some cases, the subject may be such that the structure of the paper includes several funnels in the body of the paper.

A variation of the funnel is the *pyramid*, which is a reverse funnel; you start with small details, expand into broader topics, and build to a wide base of general points. The mental gymnastics are endless. My point is not to define a rigid structure to be followed, but rather to open your thought process to consider *some* logical organization — and one with a purpose, one designed to improve the effectiveness of the writer accomplishing his objectives.

LOGICAL ARGUMENTS

A large portion of all business communications are intended to reach a conclusion or recommendation. Inherent in such a communication is the need to present an argument supporting the writer's conclusions, even if such an argument is not formalized. The recommendation may be obvious based on the material discussed and not require a great deal of debate or discussion of alternatives. But the essence of the logical development of a point of view is underlying such a communication. The concept may be easier to grasp, however, by considering the logical organization of an argumentative letter or paper with a more formalized structure.

An argument, to be effective from the writer's point of view, must persuasively *lead to the conclusions supported by the writer*. As mentioned previously, this presupposes a definite opinion on the writer's part. The organization or structure of the paper should be designed to achieve this end. It is insufficient to group ideas in a tidy fashion; the psychology of argument must also be considered and an attempt made to influence the reader's judgment by the way the paper is organized.

As in every communication, the logical structure is to have an introduction, then the body of the communication, and then some sort of summary. In the case of an argument, it is important for the introduction to clearly indicate the viewpoint of the writer. The sooner the reader knows where the writer stands, the easier it will be for him to comprehend the points made, and form his own opinion as the argument unfolds. If you doubt the importance of this, the next time you receive a lengthy letter, try jumping right in on page two.

The introduction should also form the general premise(s) for the writer's opinion and the major qualifications or limitations that will form the boundries of the argument. Virtually all communications that conclude with some recommended action could utilize this framework for an effective introduction — describe the general premise, define the boundries of the argument, and state the writer's opinion. Take the following example:

To: My Boss

PREMISE:
ONE SUPPLIER
NEEDED BY
JUNE 1

Subject: Supplier Selection for "X" Part

In accordance with the master timing plan, I have canvassed the market for potential suppliers for the "X" part to support availability by June 1, 1981. The planned volumes will require only one supplier. Quotations have been solicited and received from three companies that have the technical, manufacturing, and management capability to support the program. Based on the lowest quotation and giving due consideration to the other key factors, I believe the job should be awarded to XYZ Corporation.
I have received . . .

BOUNDRIES:
• SUPPORT VOLUME
• OTHER FACTORS
• LOW QUOTE

OPINION

Much has been written about the *psychology of argument* — the most effective way to present your case (Table 29). While open to some debate, a pattern frequently used in business is the following:

- Establish a clear point of view.
- Present any qualifying assumptions.
- Recognize the opposite point of view; concede points if necessary and refute others.
- Present points in support of your opinion; place easy to agree with things first, close with strongest argument.
- Summarize with decisive points only, that lead to a logical conclusion.

Table 29

ACCEPTED PSYCHOLOGY OF ARGUMENT

- Establish the writer's point of view clearly.
- Present any qualifying assumptions.
- Recognize the opposite point of view.
- Present points in support of writer's opinion.
- Close with strongest arguments.
- Summarize decisively to form logical conclusion.

This structure has proven to be effective and can be used to handle almost any situation. It is similar to the format frequently espoused for a persuasive debate — statement of the case, recognize the opposition, present the defense, and save the strongest arguments for last. This latter point should be considered from the reader's weighting. The writer should consider the reader's background, likely biases, or other factors and play to them.

A variation of this structure frequently can be utilized when disagreement is unlikely. In that case, it is probably good psychology to place the points on which agreement will obviously be reached at the beginning. This will place the reader in a receptive frame of mind before he encounters more controversial points.

When recognizing the opposition, it is unnecessary to elaborate at length on his counterpoints, nor is it conducive to winning the argument. In any case, the writer should be careful to avoid letting the opposing arguments become stronger than his own. It is wise to concede counter-arguments as early as possible, and to quickly refute those that are implausible in the writer's opinion. Such discussion should not be overextended relative to the length of the positive discussion, nor should the number of negative points exceed the number of positive points. The logical approach is to counterbalance the weight of positive and negative arguments, with the scale tipping in favor of the writer's viewpoint.

The positive arguments are the heart of the letter or paper. If possible, each significant point should be developed in a separate paragraph for maximum emphasis — even if such paragraphs are rather short. Organize the points in a logical sequence.

If the points follow in a straight line such that A is reinforced by B and then by C, use that order. If the points are independent, consider which would be most persuasive to the reader, and order the points with the weakest first and the strongest last.

If a routine order of discussion exists in your business, study it to see if it is appropriate for the task at hand. For example, my company, when making a major product decision, likes to discuss the market first, then competitive information, then any technical issues and finally the financial implications. The logical thing to do is to use a familiar format for maximum receptivity, unless you have a good reason for deviating from the norm. Whatever the situation, the central point is to carefully consider a logical organization of the material in the body of the communication.

Finally, the writer can use the *summary* effectively to reinforce the argument. Whenever possible, only the main points of the positive arguments should be mentioned in the summary. It weakens the conclusion to resummarize the negative points, and it is deadly to allow negative concessions or counter-arguments to appear for the first time in the summary — the reader is left wondering what else may have been left out.

It reinforces the entire paper, also, to carefully tie the conclusion back to the introduction. A clear statement of the writer's recommendations and a specific statement indicating what the writer wants the reader to do about the recommendations are logical conclusions to a tightly written argumentative paper. At this point, you may begin to appreciate the meaning of *orchestrating the logic* — the writer must have a plan to strategically present his case.

Before moving on, it is interesting to consider what makes one argument persuasive and another ineffective. In a business environment, few things can be presented that can be accepted as positive proof that a course of action is desirable. Business for the most part is a social science, not a physical science. It is incumbent on the writer to convince the reader of the "truth" of his opinion. One aspect of achieving this end is to consider the weight of the alternative arguments, as mentioned earlier. Another approach may be to assume the reader will accept the viewpoint supported by the most evidence (real or implied facts); another by the one that is the fairest, or the most logical, or the most clearly stated. The writer should *have an approach in mind* before he begins writing. In the end, the most persuasive argument will stem from an honest conviction on the part of the writer of the merits of his opinion.

LOGIC THROUGH GRAMMAR

In an earlier chapter, we discussed the notion that following accepted grammatical fundamentals was the key to accomplishing the objectives for effective writing. This is certainly true in the case of effectively orchestrating the logic of a paper. The reader, after all, will have to deduce the writer's *intended* logic from what he reads. This goes beyond simply the way the paper is organized, although it begins there. The organization is conveyed to the reader partially by good formatting techniques, as discussed earlier, and partially by the structure of the sentences and paragraphs in the text.

It is important to understand the logical use of paragraphs. They are more than a temporary break for the reader to rest his eyes or catch his breath. They have a purpose. They serve to organize the presentation of ideas from a random thought process into a cohesive, logical sequence. Common characteristics of a good paragraph are:

Table 30

COMMON CHARACTERISTICS OF GOOD PARAGRAPHS

- Unity — A central point, introduced by a topic sentence, to which each sentence is related.

- Consistency — In voice, logic, number.

- Order — The logical sequence of sentences and organization (small to large, first to last, oldest to newest, least important to most important, etc.).

- Coherence — Sentences linked together, providing clues as to the organization (First, . . ., Secondly, . . .; However, . . ., Moreover, . . ., In fact, . . ., Of course, . . .) or the relationship of the sentences (pronoun links, such as it, they, etc.; use of sentence hooks).

The importance of the continuity and logic of linking *adjacent* paragraphs is even greater than the clues left within the body of each paragraph. If each paragraph has unity, then the relationship of one paragraph to the next must be clarified — it should introduce a new thought, but is it the writer's intent to change the subject, or add a new thought to the previous subject? Such clues for the reader are referred to as *hooks*, and their mastery is the essence of good style and effective writing.

HOOKS CONVEY LOGIC

Hooks are connecting words or phrases used at the end of one paragraph and the beginning of the next paragraph to connect the two paragraphs. They are *transitional devices* to help the reader follow the main thought. They can be made up of key words that show the flow. An example is the use of *hooks* to begin this paragraph, which was left dangling as the key word in the last sentence of the previous paragraph.

Another approach is to use *standard connections*. When conceding an opponents point, for example, the paragraph may begin, "Admittedly, . . ." Or when introducing a counterpoint, the paragraph may begin, "Nevertheless, . . ." To continue a previous thought and add a new point, a paragraph may begin, "In addition,. . ." A good list of standard connections follows:

Table 31	
STANDARD CONNECTIONS AS PARAGRAPH HOOKS (Also used as sentence hooks)	
Purpose	**Connector**
Agreement	Accordingly, assuredly, clearly, thus, therefore, in fact, consequently, no doubt, obviously, unquestionably, of course, surely
Contrast	But, yet, however, nevertheless, on the other hand, after all, notwithstanding, still the fact remains
Concession	Admittedly, true, undoubtedly, granted, certainly, nobody claims, it is true that
Continuation	And, furthermore, in addition, moreover, indeed, even so, besides, next, finally, likewise, also, again
Comparison	Similarly, as discussed previously, likewise, by the same token, in like manner
Time or Place	In the meantime, meanwhile, afterward, soon, here, adjacent to, formerly, behind, in front of, opposite to
Summary, Repeat	In sum, summing up, in summary, in brief, as has been noted, for example, for instance, in fact, in conclusion

Hooks can be used to interrelate several paragraphs, to reach into the middle of the previous paragraph for closer examination, to broaden or narrow the scope of the previous thought, or any number of transitional purposes. Standard connectors may have insufficient power to satisfy all of these needs. The device used in their place is to use key phrases, words or thoughts from the previous paragraph(s) in the introductory sentence of the new paragraph. This is a subtle craft that really separates the men from the boys. Too many references of previous material, too much repetition, is insulting to the reader and distracting. If the hook is too weak, it may be ambiguous and lose the reader. Ear and experience are required for a writer to become proficient in the use of hooks and more about hooks will be discussed in the chapter on style. Suffice it to say that hooks give organization to the use of paragraphs, which provides the means for orchestrating the logic.

In addition to hooks, logic can be conveyed through attention to other fundamental "rules" of good grammar discussed in Chapters 1 and 2. For example, we discussed the need to complete comparisons logically to avoid ambiguous interpretations:

- The girls in Texas are more beautiful than California.   To be more beautiful than a state is illogical.

- The girls in Texas are more beautiful than *those in* California.   Clear comparison

Other forms of incomplete logic similar to comparisons are:

- When suggesting other alternatives exist, state at least one.

- If an idea is suggested, finish the statement of the idea.

- If more is to be said about a topic later, tell the reader it will be coming.

In general, test your writing for logical completeness. Another fundamental conducive to orchestrating the logic is to maintain a *consistent perspective* throughout the sentences and preferably throughout the entire composition:

- From my vantage point, I could see the quail flush, and the deer on the other side of the hill scampered away.

  Illogical: I could not see what was happening over the hill.

- From my vantage point, I could see the quail flush and *I was sure the deer on the other side of the hill would scamper away.*

  Logical: I could deduce what the deer might do.

It is easy to loose *perspective* in the haste of writing, and the conscientious writer will carefully reread his work to root out all illogical arguments, meanings, or constructions.

```
┌─────────────────────────────────────────┐
│                Table 32                   │
│                                           │
│      OBJECTIVES FOR GOOD ORGANIZATION     │
│                                           │
│          • Focus the content              │
│                                           │
│          • Plan the format                │
│                                           │
│          • Orchestrate the logic          │
└─────────────────────────────────────────┘
```

This chapter highlights several important concepts to consider when planning the logic of a business communication. Effective writing depends on such logical organization. Together with carefully focusing the content and planning the most effective format, orchestrating the logic will form the basis for the most persuasive organization of the material to accomplish the writer's objectives (Table 32). But the task is only beginning — the remaining chapters of this book will deal with the task of actually writing the text; the remaining writing objectives focus on the means to improve persuasiveness through effective writing techniques. By following the fundamentals and devoting some time to organizing the focus, format and logic of his (or her) writing, the ambitious businessman has gained important tools to help him move up the ladder. With a few more tools he may go further than he ever dreamed.

SECTION THREE

OBJECTIVES TO IMPROVE

PERSUASIVENESS

6

FOR EFFECTIVE WRITING

BE ABSOLUTELY CLEAR

THE *Wall Street Journal*, a deadly serious newspaper given occasionally to light hearted moments, in a November, 1979 issue, ran an article headlined "Employers Prioritize Utilization of Words to Impact Quality." The article went on to translate that many employers, as well as numerous prominent business schools, were emphasizing the need for improving business communications. The need to "promote clear, concise business writing," to avoid "pompous prose and jargon," and to generally upgrade the writing skills of the average businessman is widely recognized. Of course, other fields of endeavor outside of business circles are not immune. One professional spoofer of bureaucracy, James Boren, has offered to serve as the running mate of any presidential candidate based on his own assessment of his primary qualification: "I can profundify simplicity at the drop of an issue."

David W. Ewing, the eminent executive director of Harvard Business Review, wrote a biting article published in major newspapers with the screaming headline: "The Modern Art of Rotten Writing." His half-humorous explanation for much of the bad writing, particularly in business, was that the writer's psychology kept getting in the way. Ambiguous statements reflected a timid sole, or a rambling dissertation revealed underlying sexual frustration. He also supposed that businessmen were being heavily influenced by their expanding interface (a beautiful word) with government, and have adopted the heavy-handed, jargonfilled style of their counterparts. Why else would Checker

Motors explain to the New York Times: "It was the judgment of the board that, because it was uncertain as to whether certain matters could be determined in order to assure consummation of the transaction by year end, it was advisable to discontinue negotiations at this time in order to avoid the incurrence of additional corporate expense."

The common grounds for these articles, and hundreds of others, are the rapidly declining writing skills in business (and other sectors) and the apparent malaise regarding a solution. The malaise is being confronted importantly in influential business schools where future managers are being groomed. The pressing need is for the business community to aggressively address the issue as well. In terms of sheer numbers, those presently in business with weak writing skills and those that will enter business without the benefit of formal business education or adequate training in writing at the high school or university level, will greatly outweigh the relatively small number receiving good writing training. A few large, progressive companies are filling this void with new programs. Most are not. What an opportunity for ambitious people to seize the initiative, and either elevate themselves above the crowd by honing their writing skills through self-effort, or by influencing their companies to begin a more comprehensive program. Hopefully, this book can lead a few in this direction and form the framework for such programs.

The essential framework for developing more effective writing skills is to define and understand the *writing objectives* that have virtually universal application. We began our discussion with a review of the fundamentals as an appropriate first objective. The three objectives relating to improving the organization of written communications also have universal application. The need to focus the content, to plan the format, and to orchestrate the logic are basic criteria for effective writing. Many experienced writers incorporate these concepts into their work without conscious effort. It is habitual, and slows them down very little; in fact, their writing efficiency is probably much higher than the disorganized thinker.

The remainder of this book will be devoted to the craft of writing persuasively; that is, writing in a manner most likely to convince the reader that the writer's opinion is credible. The writing skills to achieve this end can be learned, and if diligently practiced, an ear for effective writing can be developed, just as a musician masters the violin with sufficient practice. The process begins with a recognition of five basic objectives, that when coupled with good organization, will improve the persuasive presentation of ideas. The objectives are:

Table 33

OBJECTIVES FOR WRITING PERSUASIVELY

- To be absolutely clear,

- To emphasize strategically,

- To select an appropriate tone,

- To tailor your style, and

- To write efficiently.

If you reread the list carefully and think about it, these objectives are self-explanatory. The thing that is missing is *how*. How is clarity achieved? How is strategic emphasis achieved? How is tone or style established? How can I write more efficiently? With a little effort, these questions can be answered.

This chapter will discuss how to better achieve the first objective — to be absolutely clear. Principles to be discussed are:

Table 34

PRINCIPLES FOR WRITING CLEARLY

- Critique all writing from the reader's standpoint.
- Avoid unclear sentence structure.
- Avoid faulty pronoun reference.
- Avoid misplaced modifiers.
- Avoid faulty parallelism.
- Consider semantics precisely.
- Use figures of speech cautiously.
- Avoid useless jargon.
- Avoid idiomatic expressions.
- Avoid acronyms.
- Follow accepted grammar fundamentals.

It is easy to say, "Be absolutely clear." But, in practice, this is one of the more difficult objectives to achieve. No one sets out to be unclear. The writer probably is convinced he has been clear all along. Improvement in this area requires a very penetrating, questioning review of your work, always from the reader's standpoint. The use of the fundamentals covered in Chapters 1 and 2, of course, are basic to achieving clarity. Proper spelling, punctuation, and sentence structure all are required to clearly express ideas. In addition, certain frequently encountered mistakes can be discussed; elimination of just these few things would improve the vast majority of communications.

The first general area that may reduce clarity is the lack of fundamental sentence construction. In order to write clear sentences, it is necessary to avoid constructions that are ambiguous, misleading, or illogical. Such problems are frequently the result of either faulty pronoun reference, misrelated modifiers, or faulty parallelism.

FAULTY PRONOUN REFERENCES

As we covered briefly in the chapters on fundamentals, it is necessary for pronouns to *agree* with their antecedent in person, gender, and number. Disagreement can be confusing and gives the impression the writer has lost his way. The mistake is seldom encountered when the pronoun is used in close proximity to the antecedent; in long rambling sentences with several pronouns being used, however, it is very common. In addition, many antecedents can become complex in structure, making it difficult to know what form of the pronoun to use. The inexperienced writer should explore the use and misuse of pronouns thoroughly in a good grammar book, and when in doubt while writing, stop and refer to a reference book for assistance. Clarity is too important to treat pronouns casually.

Another difficulty encountered in pronoun references, other than agreement, is the *remoteness* of the reference, or the lack of a direct linkage to the antecedent. This is particularly prevalent when using the ambiguous "this." If used to refer to a general thought that has been developed by using several sentences, *this* may become ambiguous; it may also be confused with reference to a sub-idea of the general thought, or it may be interpreted in several ways by the reader. *This* is a particularly strong and useful pronoun; it saves much effort in restating or paraphrasing a general idea, and if used carefully, is perfectly acceptable. However, it is easy to misuse *this* — again, the flow of thought that is clear to the writer, may not be as clear to the reader. Whenever *this* is encountered when writing, or reading, it should become a caution flag; it should mean "watch out." Always reread the text to be sure only one antecedent reference is logically possible.

MISPLACED MODIFIERS

Modifiers are necessary to clearly express the limits of a thought; however, they can destroy clarity if not handled with care. Whenever a sentence includes two or more words that the modifier might relate to, the placement of the modifier becomes crucial to clarity:

- John talked while I studied *in whispers*.

- John talked *in whispers* while I studied.

Another common problem related to modifiers is the ambiguous structure of a *squinting modifier*. This results when the modifier is so located in the sentence that it could refer to either of two parts of the sentence:

- People who get drunk *frequently* disgrace themselves.

Is *getting drunk frequently* the disgrace?
Or, do drunks *frequently disgrace themselves*?

Does frequently modify drunk or disgrace?

Without belaboring the point, it should be sufficient to caution the inexperienced writer to first recognize when a modifier is being used, and, secondly, to be certain that it is clearly joined to the word or phrase being modified.

FAULTY PARALLELISM

As discussed earlier, the concept of parallelism is prevalent in writing — more so in business communications, probably, than in novels or other forms of writing. The concept is encountered when trying to express a series of ideas that are related in some manner, or when expressing compound subjects and predicates, or when using coordinating conjunctions with phrases, or when making comparisons. In all these cases, skillful writing is required to assure clear, logical construction of the sentence. The following examples show the numerous mistakes that can be made in parallel construction resulting in illogical meanings, ambiguous interpretations, or simply poor style (lack of rhythm and balance):

Parallel Series
- Faulty: The boss asked for a copy of the paper and that his secretary should arrange for the meeting.

- Clearer: The boss asked his secretary *to make* a copy of the paper and *to arrange* for the meeting.

Parallel Series
- Faulty: The meeting was called to approve the program, decide what funding is required, and engineering reported on the test status.

- Clearer: The meeting was called *to approve* the program, *to decide* what funding is required, and *to have* engineering report on the test status.

Faulty Parallelism Through Misuse of Coordinating Conjunctions
- Faulty: The manager finished the paper and without mistakes.

- Clearer: The manager finished the paper without mistakes.

Parallel Agreement Following Coordinating Conjunction
- Faulty: The foreman returned to the shop, and the workers *will go* on strike.

- Clearer: The foreman returned to the shop, and the workers *went* on strike.

Parallel Use Of Compound Predicates
- Faulty: George is a salesman and who has been an accountant.

- Clearer: George is a salesman *and has* previously *been* an accountant.

Parallel Balance In Comparisons
- Faulty: The report is not only disorganized, but it is also too brief.

- Clearer: The report is not only *too disorganized*, but also *too brief*.

Good parallel style will improve effectiveness by making the ideas clear and emphatic. The concept is to carefully use the same grammatical construction for each idea when combining more than one thought in the same sentence. The neophite, however, can become mesmerized by parallelism. In many cases, it is better to consider separating the thoughts into several sentences. It becomes a matter of judgment. As in most stylistic considerations, the "ear" of the writer should dictate the form.

SEMANTICS

In addition to sound sentence construction, another area of concentration necessary for achieving the objective of being absolutely clear is the area of semantics — understanding the exact meaning of words. In business, it is unnecessary to be a semanticist of the caliber of a Spiro Agnew, or even a William Buckley. In fact, just the opposite — it is better to use the simplest words in your lexicon, as long as the words express exactly what you intend. Pompous prose is just that — pompous. Most businessmen deplore reading material in which the writer forces the use of "big" words. It impresses no one and may disrupt the reader if he does not know the meaning.

It is important, however, to make the effort to find the exact word to express an idea accurately. Some words *denote* a precise idea. The word "tree" has a clear meaning. The word "car" likewise is clear, even though many types of cars exist. Other words express a general idea — they have a relatively vague meaning. Words like landscaping and transportation are certainly less precise than tree or car. Edward Thompson, Editor-in-Chief for *Readers Digest,* refers to "first-degree" words, versus words that must be translated before a clear image comes to mind. "Book" is a first-degree word, whereas "publication" is not. Whenever possible, it is better to utilize first-degree words to achieve clarity.

Many words either denote an actual image, or *connote* an implied meaning. When someone is referred to as being a "dog" it obviously is not to be taken as a literal reference to the animal. Likewise, the word "road" can be specific in some situations, but may have many connotations if not further described to the reader. If it is necessary to have precise understanding of the circumstances, the writer may need to explain whether the road is paved or muddy. If the writer tells the reader "the car is careening down a deeply rutted, muddy road precariously winding its way along the edge of the mountain," the connotation is much more clear than if he refers simply to a "car careening down a mountain road." It is important for writers to distinguish between the denotation of words and their connotations to clearly express the intended thoughts.

FIGURES OF SPEECH

Whereas words may connote different things to different people, likewise a body of English referred to as "figures of speech" has evolved to express ideas through the images they connote, rather than their literal meanings. The usage of such grammar is invaluable to give a more *concrete* meaning to generalities, and if used judiciously, they can be better than a much longer, wordy description to accomplish the same thing. Most people understand what it means to be "on the ball," or to eat to your "heart's content," but try to express these ideas without using a figure of speech. In business, it can be distracting to resort to flowery prose or overly trite expressions, but nevertheless, in many situations improved clarity, as well as more efficient writing, can result from carefully using expressions that will be meaningful to the reader.

Figures of speech are caregorized as follows:

Table 35

Figures Of Speech

Figure of Speech	Usage	Example
• Simile	Explicit comparison between two things (introduced with "like" or "as").	He was as quiet as a mouse.
• Metaphor	An implied comparison.	He was a bear of a man.
• Personification	To personify an inanimate object	The good Mother Earth will provide.
• Metonymy	Use the name of one thing for that of another.	The pitcher fired that apple.
• Synecdoche	Use a part to stand for the whole, or vice versa.	He had ten head. (cattle)
• Litotes	An understatement, meaning the maximum of the opposite.	Babe Ruth was not a bad ball player.
• Hyperbole	Deliberate overstatement.	The umpire was blind.
• Allusion	An indirect reference to a well recognized example.	He was the Woody Hayes of his field.
• Common Expressions	Catch phrase, using normal word meanings.	We agreed to disagree. He was the center of attention.

The problem with using figures of speech in business correspondence is that they frequently seem out of place. The tone of the letter changes and credibility may be reduced. It is better to avoid such tempting phrases unless they directly improve clarity. In this context, similes and metaphors can be useful because they can connote concrete images if handled skillfully. In business, however, they should be used sparingly, and then only after carefully considering the audience.

BUSINESS JARGON

At the other extreme of using informal figures of speech is the heavy handed, formal business jargon so prevalent in business communications. In response to the widespread misuse of jargon, Harvard Business School initiated a new course with primary emphasis on attacking this problem. Other prominent business schools have also strengthened their courses in this regard. Such guidance will come too late for the multitudes already occupied in business; their best defense is to gain a sensitivity to avoiding the obtuse phraseology they have grown up with and ruthlessly control the efforts of their subordinates and themselves. It starts with a recognition that wordiness seldom adds to clarity, but rather detracts from it.

Jargon is defined by Webster's New Collegiate Dictionary as:

- Obscure and often pretentious language marked by circumlocutions and long words.

- Technical terminology or characteristic idiom of a special activity.

- Confused unintelligible language.

Each definition is valid in a business context. In most cases, all three are germane to the same piece of writing. Who can possibly decipher, "The Technical Verification and Assessment Committee formalized the inter-face labor-wise for facilitizing to achieve feedback that conceptualizes the learning curve for thru-put of the commonized data that when finalized will maximize the committee's thrust funding-wise." My files are full of "-ize issums" and "-wise issums," as well as many other vocabulary inventions. The later chapter on writing efficiently will discuss avoidance of these and other forms of jargon in more detail. Jargon can be captivating for the writer, but unless he is consistently reminded that clarity is the overriding objective, the mesmerizing effect of voluminous prose can dominate his writing and undermine the effectiveness of the communication.

IDIOMS

Idioms are a form of jargon, or perhaps may be considered *figures of speech* in many commonly used phrases; however, idioms can be a useful form of shorthand to communicate effectively. In the proper context, it can be sufficient to suggest a meeting "to conclude the deal", rather than say, " . . . to execute our signatures on the aforementioned contract." Likewise, "To strike a bargain" is an idiom that leaves little room for ambiguous interpretation; it is unnecessary to say, "to reach a mutually satisfactory agreement that is equitable to each party." On the other hand, thousands of idiomatic expressions have crept into the English language and not all have clear connotations.

Clarity demands that the business writer use idioms with caution. An idiom can be any commonly used phrase that has meaning peculiar to a special group, which often cannot be interpreted literally. *Dialectical language* can be idiomatic — a southerner may feel comfortable writing about buying a car "off of" a client, whereas, others may use simply "from." Fuzzy cliches, such as "foreseeable future" are also idiomatic and are best avoided. In business, however, many of the idioms are a result of special purpose language. Brokers refer to "margin purchases." Air conditioning engineers relate to competitive "pull-down performance." Every occupation is raft with idioms, or jargon, peculiar to their own field. The problem in correspondence usually arises from transferring expressions from one field of business to another, or from one function (engineering) to another (marketing) within the same company. The writer must always consider the audience and be sure they will be as familiar with the idiom as he is, or clear understanding will breakdown.

One further caution on using idioms, figures of speech, and certain jargon phrases: If you must use these phrases, get them right. Misquoting a phrase is at a minimum humorous and distracting; at its worst, it can be confusing and destroy clarity. It's "in accordance with," not, "in accordance to." It's "prior to," not "prior than." You could be "caught on the horns of a dilemma," but to refer to "the other horn of the dilemma" is inaccurate and could be confusing. You don't "*convince* somebody *to* act," you "*convince* somebody *that*," or "*convince* somebody *of*". You can be considered "an intellectual tour de *farce*" if you happen to misspell *force*. If you attempt to be light and airy, it can be disastrous if the jargon is inaccurate. When in doubt, consult a good Thesaurus or other reference source.

ACRONYMS

A special concern relative to achieving clear communications must be raised regarding the prevalent use and misuse of acronyms in business (UAW, NAACP, ERA, UPCIPAC, etc.). A frequent mistake is to assume the audience is conversant with the jargon of the writer, particularly in the use of such abbreviations. This is particularly noticeable when one function (engineering) is communicating to another function (finance or marketing) within the same company, or when two companies in different fields of business are communicating. Unless certain that the audience will recognize the acronyms, the writer is best advised to spell out the words, at least the first time they are used in the communication. This is particularly important the further away the audience is organizationally, or in terms of background, from the writer's own experience.

FOLLOW THE FUNDAMENTALS

No chapter on achieving clarity would be complete without a reminder that the fundamentals of good grammar are all directed toward this end. A summary of the key fundamentals through which clarity can be achieved is shown in Table 36. It's difficult to convince the average businessman that the familiar sentence structure and bad habits he has developed over the years can really be reducing the effectiveness of his communications. From his viewpoint, he may believe his business is being accomplished, and therefore, his writing habits are of little concern to him. However, he is probably the same individual that is mystified by the success of others as he watches them progress up the ladder. He will never know what his full potential may have been, since he is competing with an important weakness in his armament. Would a better understanding of grammar fundamentals (and the other elements of good writing) have made the critical difference? A thoughtful person with an ambition to succeed will not risk the answer to this question.

Table 36

KEY GRAMMAR FUNDAMENTALS RELATED TO WRITING CLEARLY

- Spot and correct dangling modifiers.
- Do not omit necessary words, particularly for comparisons.
- Use the proper adjective and adverb form for the intended meaning —
  positive (cold), comparative (colder — between two), or superlative (coldest
  — more than two).
- Use commas properly to avoid confusion for:
  - non-restrictive modifiers and appositives
    (George Washington, our first President, . . .)
  - sentence modifiers
  - contrasted sentence elements
  - introductory adverbial clauses
  - introductory verbal phrases
  - adjectives out of normal order
    (A man, powerful and dangerous, did . . .)
  - other words or phrases that interrupt the sentence
  - to avoid misreading
    (All that he has, has been pledged.)
- Correct fused sentences, erroneously joined with a comma:
  - use a period (make two sentences)
  - use a semicolon
  - join with a coordinating conjunction
  - use a subordinating conjunction
- Use dashes or parenthesis to clearly set off extraneous material,
  supplemental ideas, or for a very abrupt transition of thought.
- Hyphenate words to avoid ambiguity or to join two words used as a single
  adjective.
  - The dark-brown dress was becoming.
  - He re-created the drawing.
  - The haunted mansion was thrill-less.

The process of persuasion begins with achieving a clear understanding between the writer and the readers of his work. The tools to achieve such clarity are the choice of appropriate words to exactly express the desired thoughts, and the organization of such words, together with appropriate punctuation, into sentences and paragraphs that clearly connote only one interpretation. When individual words are insufficient to permit an accurate picture, phrases or figures of speech may facilitate a more concrete understanding. Judgment and experience are required to recognize when the writer is using superfluous words, or has entered the realm of pompous prose and unnecessary jargon, resulting from a misguided desire to impress an audience. Clarity and, therefore, possibly persuasion, can be sacrificed on the alter of ego satisfaction unless the writer has clear objectives in mind.

7

FOR EFFECTIVE WRITING
EMPHASIZE STRATEGICALLY

PERSUASIVE writing can be greatly enhanced through appropriate emphasis — emphasis strategically planned by the author during the organization of his work and accomplished during the process of writing his material. This objective, *to emphasize strategically*, is the most overlooked objective discussed in this book, and, as any skilled writer knows, it is of primary importance in persuading the reader. Similarly, the most effective lawyers know that emphasis is a key courtroom skill to be effective. Businessmen, just as lawyers, when in oral debates, use body language, gestures, voice inflections and decibel levels to reinforce the desired emphasis of key points. Communicating in writing, however, depends on other factors to achieve emphasis.

On numerous occasions, I can recall my boss commenting, "It's got the ideas I wanted; but — I don't know — it doesn't pop out the key point we're trying to make. That key idea you mentioned to me doesn't leap out at me. It's not bad, but let's see if we can change the emphasis slightly to bring the point out front." After years of dealing with requests to rewrite my draft material, I now know mechanically how to change my text to establish the desired *emphasis*. To the inexperienced writer, *emphasis* may seem like a nebulous word, and initially he may be mystified as to how to achieve it. This chapter is intended to convey certain principles for achieving desired emphasis as a basis for learning how to modify your own writing as the situation requires.

Emphasis is largely controlled at the discretion of the writer by considering four areas of writing techniques:

Table 37

WRITING TECHNIQUES TO CONTROL EMPHASIS

- Logical organization
- Selection and use of verbs
- Sentence structure
- Formatting techniques

Although other elements of grammar or writing techniques could add or detract from manipulating the emphasis desired by the writer, concentrating on these four areas will resolve most situations encountered. These are sufficiently powerful tools to transform average writing into excellent writing.

LOGICAL ORGANIZATION

Chapter 5 was entirely devoted to the importance of planning whatever is being written to assure a logical flow of argument and organization. Several points bear repeating in the context of organizing to achieve appropriate emphasis of key points. First, the writer needs to be clear in his own mind what he wants to emphasize. For example, when several arguments are being presented to support a position, it is incumbent on the writer to determine which are least important (or least persuasive) and which are strongest. It is insufficient to simply list the arguments in random order. It is irresponsible to make the reader decide which are most important, and certainly contrary to the writer's own interests to abdicate the control. Maximum emphasis, of course, should be given to the strongest points.

In addition, as we discussed earlier, the organization should be clear to the reader. Assuming the writer has planned a logical development of his paper, he must also assure that the reader is following along with him, step by step, as intended. Several writing techniques to achieve this were described and emphasis can be achieved in the same manner. A consistent flow of least to most, first to last, etc., plus the concepts of parallel structure, paragraph hooks, and transitional connectors or phrases, all apply to controlling the reader's comprehension of the logic the author is establishing. When it becomes time to emphasize, the reader should be following right along and be prepared for it.

For maximum effectiveness, the location of the key points to be emphasized is critical. Within a composition, the *last* paragraph or argument is usually given more weight by the reader, since it is the last thought encountered. Theoreticians and psychologists may debate this (possibly *first* is strongest, since everything that follows is related to it), but I am satisfied that "strongest, last" works based on my experience in a business environment. Likewise, within a paragraph, the last sentence should carry more weight, and its emphasis will be greater than the other sentences simply due to its position. Within a sentence, the key words or phrases should also be carefully considered for maximum emphasis. Placing them at the end is always effective; however, the initial words can have emphatic importance as well.

Weak:
> You could become a skilled writer through carefully studying this book.

Emphatic:
> Careful study of this book will make you a skilled writer.

Another consideration in organizing your thoughts to improve emphasis is to restrain from overstating your case. Occasionally excessive detail in explaining a point results in actually obscuring the central idea and emphasis is lost. Even if the point is clearly made, too much reinforcing information may result in suspicion on the reader's part (the "me thinks thou doest protest too strongly" syndrome). Likewise, the use of exaggerations — *disastrous consequences, mandatory, unquestionably, ultimate*, and the like — can easily reduce credibility, rather than imparting the desired emphasis, unless used with discretion.

The clearest way to achieve emphasis is to simply tell the reader what you are emphasizing. A phrase such as, "most importantly, . . ." or, "the main point is . . ." can accomplish directly what a more subtle approach may not. Summation phrases can also assist the reader to find the emphatic points — "Based on this last point, clearly . . ." or, "I am persuaded by the fact . . ." or, "In my opinion, the above arguments show . . ." Incidentally, an indisputable *fact* is usually more convincing, and thus more emphatic, than an opinion. It is helpful (and greatly improves credibility) to distinguish the difference for the reader. A skillful writer will leave many clues for the reader to catch the desired emphasis, including actually telling him.

SELECTION OF VERBS — ACTIVE AND PASSIVE VOICE

In the earlier chapter regarding fundamentals, the difference between *active* and *passive* voice was briefly defined. We now need to examine why such a distinction is important. Most sentences could be constructed either way. That is because most verbs can be either active or passive depending upon their use in a particular sentence.

The wind *parted* my hair. (Active)

My hair *was parted* by the wind. (Passive)

It is fundamental to recognize the difference in order to use the different forms to your advantage. Refresh your memory as often as necessary until you can spot the passive voice in your own writing or when reading the writing of someone else. It is of primary importance in establishing appropriate emphasis.

An active verb makes the subject do something; whereas a passive verb always forces the subject to be acted upon. With this in mind, it should be simply a matter of the author knowing what he *intends* and then using the proper verb form. If you intend for the subject to act, use active voice. The emphasis of the sentence will thus be consistent with the intent. If your purpose is to have the subject acted upon, choose the passive voice to achieve the appropriate emphasis.

Many respected writing authorities admonish their students to avoid passive voice, except as a last resort. They frequently use examples of business writing, e.g., minutes of meetings, to demonstrate how dry and lifeless prose becomes when passive voice is predominately used.

> The minutes were read by the Secretary and unanimously approved. The agenda was reviewed by the Chairman. The first report was given by Finance and after lengthy discussion was tabled. Etc., etc., etc.

How true, lifeless. No one is acting, and yet during the meeting, the Secretary, Chairman, Finance, etc., were doing something. Each sentence could be rewritten to indicate action. I won't belabor the point with an example of minutes of a meeting. After all, minutes are usually written for the record only and not to influence, persuade, or even emphasize. Then too, something can be said in favor of convention and tradition. If minutes were written like a soap opera, it would probably cause much consternation and distraction at executive levels, at least initially, and serve little purpose. Many other areas of business correspondence, however, could stand a shot of adrenalin from the use of active voice, and more importantly, the author would regain control of the emphasis he desires.

A good guideline to follow is to always use active voice, except in the following three instances:

1. When the subject should be acted upon

2. When the sentence explains something about the subject

3. When the author elects to break the rhythm for better style.

Let's examine these exceptions in more detail. The first is simple to understand, but it sings a siren song. It is tempting to rationalize the use of passive voice for this reason without considering the resultant emphasis. For maximum emphasis, normally it is most effective to have the subject act. Occasions do arise, however, where the opposite can be true. If a calamity has befallen the subject, it can be more emphatic to state that he was acted upon.

A shot killed the man.	Active
The man was killed by a shot.	Passive, more emphatic

or

A strike closed the plant.	Active
The plant was closed by a strike.	Passive

In the latter example, the best form may depend on the context in which the sentence is being used. If the emphasis should be on the *strike*, the first sentence, with the active verb, may be better. If the discussion, however, is primarily about the *plant*, e.g., why it lost production in the second quarter, the second sentence keeps the emphasis on the plant, where it belongs. The point to be made is that the author should *consciously decide* which subject he wants to emphasize and structure the sentence accordingly. More emphasis inherently is attributed to the subject of the sentence than to the object, and the author selects the subject through his use of verbs. This is a fundamental way to control emphasis.

A second exception to the use of active voice frequently derives from the need to *explain something* about the subject. The most sensible structure in this case would be to have the *thing* being explained about as the subject of the sentence, with the object of the sentence made up of the explanation.

Example:
>   Passive voice *is formed* by combining some form of the verb "to be" with the past participle of another verb.

Active voice would be awkward and less effective:

Example:
>   Combining some form of the verb "to be" with the past participle of another verb *forms* the passive voice.

The third reason for considering the use of passive voice is simply to alter the rhythm of a paragraph. Here again, this can become a tempting excuse for a lazy writer, but if used conscientiously, passive voice can soften the tone, slow down the action, result in a pause for emphasis, or otherwise breakup a steady stream of active verbs. Stylistic use of passive voice is difficult to master, however, and when rereading your text, it is wise to second-guess such usage. Try to reconstruct the passive sentence to use an active verb, and if you don't like the result, forget it. Always be suspicious of two verbs followed with "by" — a dead give away of passive voice. When encountered, think about it. If emphasis would be improved by changing the sentence, make the change. If not, move on. It becomes a matter of judgment and "ear." If it sounds right to you in the context of the paragraph, passive voice may be best.

A final thought on the selection of verbs to gain the desired emphasis: whenever possible, use concrete, action verbs, rather than vague, multi-purpose words. Words that convey a sound or a picture of the specific action are more effective than general words. For example:

- Use *sprint*, rather than went
- Use *beg*, rather than ask
- Use *strive*, rather than try
- Use *crashed*, rather than fell
- Use *barked*, rather than said

Selection of verbs and their use are of primary importance in achieving emphasis. Other elements of sentence structure are also conducive to planning and controlling emphasis.

SENTENCE STRUCTURE

In the haste of writing, it is easy for the writer to carelessly misplace key points when constructing his sentences and lose the emphasis he should be carefully establishing. A fault frequently encountered is to let the main thought become part of a subordinate clause.

Faulty:
> The meeting was held yesterday, although the plan has not been approved.

Better:
> The plan has not been approved, even though the meeting was held yesterday.

Incidentally, this example is useful to demonstrate another structural way to achieve better emphasis. It is normally more emphatic to put statements in a positive form; negative expressions should be avoided. In the case above, it would be better to read:

> The plan was *rejected* (or tabled, or deferred) at yesterday's meeting.

- Use *dishonest*, rather than *not honest*.

- Use *ignored*, rather than *did not pay any attention to*.

Whenever the word "not" is encountered in your writing, see if you can find a better verb to replace it and state the same thought positively.

The placement of modifiers is another way to control emphasis. Most modifiers of verbs can be placed at will throughout the sentence and the careful writer can alter the rhythm and emphasis by strategically placing the modifier where he wants it.

> *Slowly* the bus came down the hill.

> The bus *slowly* came down the hill.

>   or,

> *Consequently*, the senator refused.

> The senator, *consequently*, refused.

The same is true for modifiers of nouns, particularly nouns having *non-restrictive* modifiers:

> Modifier placement, *which can be critical to emphasis*, must be considered strategically.

> Modifier placement must be considered strategically, *which can be critical to emphasis*.

Some words, however, connote meaning based on their location in the sentence (*only, nearly*, or *almost*) and must be used with extra care.

> *Only* he told me.

> He told me *only*.

Prepositions (*by, from, in, to*, etc.) are curious parts of speech in that their location can frequently be discretionary. In particular, placement of a preposition at the end of a sentence can be more emphatic.

Awkward:
> For what are we being paid?

Emphatic:
> What are we being paid for?

>   or,

Weak:
> We survive or fail on profits.

Emphatic:
> Profits are what we survive or fail on.

A final thought for improving emphasis that relates as much to writing style as it does to sentence structure *per se*, is regarding the use of personal pronouns (*I, you, we, his,* etc.). Frequently, in business correspondence, a writer will use phrases such as "I think . . .", "I believe . . .", "We believe . . .", or "In my opinion . . ." Unless the writer is responding to a direct request for his opinion, such phrases are actually unnecessary embellishments that distract the reader from the thought being communicated. The next time you are tempted to include such a phrase (and the temptation is usually overwhelming), consider whether the emphasis would be improved by leaving it out. Normally, a direct statement will sound more authoritative and more emphatic. An "I believe" introduction frequently smacks of being slightly apologetic. At the very least, it baits the reader with an implied, "What do you think?" A positive statement avoids tempting the reader to consider other possibilities and, thus, is more emphatic.

FORMATTING FOR EMPHASIS

The fourth area of consideration to control emphasis is through the use of formatting techniques. Chapter 4 discussed at length certain fundamentals for controlling the reader's thought process through format methods in order to accomplish the author's objectives. The format can be a strong tool for the writer to achieve the objective of emphasizing strategically as well. Beyond the overall considerations of formatting discussed in Chapter 4, which definitely plays a role in gaining emphasis for the total letter or report, very specific emphasis can be controlled by detailed considerations within the paragraphs and sentences themselves.

Punctuation marks are visual aids, really formatting tools, to convey emphasis, as well as to convey a clear understanding of a thought. In particular, *italics, quotation marks, parenthesis,* and *dashes* are useful to set off key phrases or add supplementary material for added emphasis. Look back through the last few pages of this book and find the numerous occasions I was compelled to use such a formatting technique. Was greater emphasis achieved? In the same manner, a business letter could be improved by judicious use of punctuation strictly for added emphasis. Of course, if overused, the approach has less value — not everything deserves to be emphasized, and if all key points are given the same weight through similar emphasis, the weighting is neutralized into meaninglessness.

Other primary formatting techniques for emphasis are *indenting, boxing-in* a separate statement, adding a *table* of data to support a key point, or listing key things in a *bullet point* fashion. You don't want to achieve the appearance of a Kiplinger's News Letter, which highlights everything, but a conservative use of such formats can be very effective. In particular, the *underline* should be used cautiously. It is tempting to show every instance when the writer would raise his voice if presenting his work orally. In some cases, this can be a good motive, of course, particularly with a word that has vague emphasis in itself.

> The project <u>will</u> succeed. (Implied: or else!)

Of course, none of the foregoing discussion can be utilized unless the writer has a clear idea of what he wants to emphasize. This is partially a matter of business judgment and experience. It is very much a matter of recognizing that strategic emphasis should be a fundamental objective of writing in order to be most persuasive and to improve the overall effectiveness of the written communication. Knowing what to emphasize and how to do it are primary distinctions between the writing of successful businessmen and those who struggle up the ladder, or fall off of it entirely.

8

FOR EFFECTIVE WRITING

SELECT AN APPROPRIATE TONE

WHENEVER TWO people communicate, the exchange has a *tone* about it. When two friends talk, the tone is friendly. When lovers fight, the tone is angry. In oral conversations, these tones or emotions or moods are conveyed in a wide variety of ways: from voice inflections, from facial expressions, from gestures and body language, and from the words used. Written communications are similar; a tone must be established for full understanding. However, the means for communicating the tone are limited to the visual words, punctuation, and format of the correspondence. It is difficult to write a completely toneless letter. Even the dry, lifeless minutes to a meeting have an authoritative tone about them.

For fully effective writing, the author should establish a tone to suit his own purposes, rather than allow a tone to be unwittingly established by his writing. Tone is conveyed primarily through the *selection of words* used for verbs, adjectives, adverbs and other modifying parts of speech. In addition, tone can be influenced by *sentence structure* and other grammatical considerations. For the author to take charge of his writing and consciously select a tone conducive to persuading a reader effectively, he must first recognize that establishing tone is a key objective of his writing. The choice of tone is endless:

Table 38

CHOICE OF TONE

Abrupt	Confident	Patronizing
Accommodating	Demanding	Permissive
Acrimonious	Excited	Pompous
Angry	Flippant	Positive
Apologetic	Flowery	Pretensive
Appealing	Friendly	Shrill
Argumentative	Harsh	Statesmanlike
Biased	Happy	Suggestive
Beligerant	Inquisitive	Tactful
Concilatory	Insulting	Uncertain

117

In speaking, tone is established through the choice of words used and the sound of the spoken words. Well written sentences also should have *sounds*. That is, when being read, the reader actually *hears* himself reading the words. Therefore, effective writing should sound like natural speech, but it can never fully achieve it. Speech is normally much too disorganized, and it is made understandable through all the other peripheral things a speaker does while he is talking. Consider the infamous confusion over the Nixon tapes. In printed form, they became almost unintelligible (excusing even the expletive deletions). A writer must achieve tone in a very careful and conscious manner that frequently requires strenuous mental work, struggling to find just the right word. But it is worth it.

Principles to be discussed for controlling tone are shown in Table 39.

SELECTION OF TONE

Establishing tone requires a good understanding of *semantics*. Careless selection of words and phrases can mistakenly alter the tone. Usually, numerous ways exist to express a general thought. For example, when withholding support for a proposed plan, the author might use any of the following:

Tone	Example
Tactful	The plan has merit, but we cannot support it.
Abrupt	We do not support the plan.
Harsh	The plan is unacceptable.
Weak	We do not favor the plan.
Permissive	We would not object to the plan.
Uncertain	We are concerned about the plan.
Conciliatory	The plan is marginally unacceptable.
Flippant	Are you sure this is the best plan?
Insulting	The plan is ridiculous.
Pompous	The proposed strategy lacks specificity and requires further amplification before our endorsement can be acknowledged.

Table 39

PRINCIPLES FOR CONTROLLING TONE

- Select a persuasive tone for the occasion.
- Consider connotations from the reader's standpoint.
- Avoid an uncertain tone.
- Respect the reader's intelligence.
- Make it interesting to the reader.
- Make it easy to read.

An earlier chapter discussed the fact that writing becomes a reflection of the personality holding the pen. Nowhere is this more amply demonstrated than in the selection, either consciously or unconsciously, of the tone. A reticent personality must be on guard against the insertion of words that are unnecessarily apologetic. An aggressive personality (such as most up-wardbound businessmen) must consider whether a demanding word is necessary or whether it might be more effective to accomplish his goals with a more suggestive approach.

I should appreciate your assistance, since we have not followed normal procedures in this matter.	Self-scolding

or,

I should appreciate your assistance in this matter.	Sufficient

or,

A prompt reply to our customer would be appropriate.	Demanding

or,

A prompt reply to our customer may be appropriate.	Suggestive

The point to be made in these examples is that it is incumbent on the author to *select* the desired tone through his choice of words and phrases. For maximum effectiveness, he must appreciate that a tone *is* being established, recognize what probable connotation the words will have on his audience, and manipulate the tone to persuade the reader accordingly.

AVOID UNCERTAINTY

Certain words admit a degree of uncertainty that introduces a tone of doubt into the writing. Auxiliary words such as *would, should, may, might*, and *can* should be reserved for situations involving real uncertainty. Likewise, nebulous words, such as *very* or *quite* or *almost* or *about*, result in ambiguous interpretations and an uncertain tone. It is tempting to "soften" writing with the use of such words, but care must be taken or such writing will lack authority and reduce persuasiveness.

RESPECT THE AUDIENCE

Tone can reflect the author's attitude toward his audience, as well as his own personality. A particularly damaging tone that can destroy effective communication is one that is patronizing toward the reader. Most intelligent businessmen read right through the patronizing jargon and react with varying degrees of defensive rejection or downright anger. Avoid phrases like:

> While you may not have considered, . . .
> Although I realize you are new to the territory, . . .
> It is understandable for your first attempt to . . .
> Previous experience indicates . . .
> Your arguments are sound, but perhaps you
> overlooked . . .

An effective writer must assume his audience has an intellect at least comparable to his own. If he honestly is distrustful of the reader's intelligence, patronizing phrases, overblown arguments, or superfluous writing will abound. If the reader interprets a lack of respect toward him from your words, your effectiveness will be greatly reduced. An executive who has the characteristics to be upwardbound will have a sensitivity for getting the most out of people, and this skill needs to be reflected in his writing as well.

MAKE IT INTERESTING

Another element of tone quality is making the writing interesting to the reader. Much could be written on this subject (and it is encountered in many good text books on writing), but my purpose in this book is to simply remind those interested in improving business communications that a basic element of communicating effectively is to catch the reader's attention. It is tempting to accomplish this with a bombshell introduction, a dramatic eye-catching title, or a "hot" first sentence reminiscent of advertising copy. Such gimmicks are notably ineffective. A better approach is to consider the tone, particularly the tone of the introductory paragraph and the summary paragraph. After considering the audience, establish a tone that will most likely catch his interest. Consider the fundamental aspects that make any subject interesting:

Table 40

ELEMENTS THAT CREATE INTEREST

- A benefit to the reader
- A fresh point of view
- An argumentative issue
- A challenge
- A solution to a problem
- Opposition
- Controversy
- "Newsworthy" material
- New or added information
- Timeliness

Emphasize these elements in the communication to catch the reader's attention and hold his interest. *Consciously attempt to make it interesting to the reader* — this effort is normally all it takes. Use words or phrases to point out to him or remind him why he should be interested. Reinforce it in the introduction, close, and body of the communication. It is wise to avoid taking it for granted that the reader will be as interested as you are in the content of the message. By selecting an appropriate tone, however, you can make it interesting.

MAKE IT EASY TO READ

A more subtle aspect of tone is *readability*. We have discussed the necessity to attempt to write as though the author were speaking the message, even though writing actually must be supplemented in certain ways to replace the audio and visual effects inherent in communicating orally. A well written letter, however, will be as easy to read as it would be to listen to a speaker. The reader should never have to reread a passage before full comprehension sinks in. He should never "get lost" — after reading most of the letter finding himself confused, or suprised by an unrelated thought, or wandering off on a tangential argument. But more importantly, the tone should facilitate readability: the flow of the paragraphs and sentences should have a natural cadence and *sound*.

The two extremes of awkward sound that destroy readability are the *grammar school sound* and *pompous prose*. The grammar school sound is transmitted through an unbroken series of simple sentences — subject-verb-object, possibly with a few adjectives thrown in:

> We do not support the product guidelines. The guidelines reflect a reduction in overall size. The guidelines reflect a reduction in overall weight. But the guidelines are targeted only two years away. The products must last for five years. If they do not, profit objectives will not be met. The guidelines should be targeted five years away. In five years, a greater reduction in size and weight will be necessary. Therefore, we do not support the product guidelines.

Such a choppy tone becomes difficult to tolerate. In addition, because the points become spread out, it is difficult for the reader to quickly grasp the central point. The other extreme, pompous prose, is equally difficult to follow:

> Of paramount importance in our deliberations regarding the propriety of the subject guidelines that will dictate the future destiny of our products was a comprehensive consideration of the appropriate strategic time-frame within which the said products must remain viable. Profitability objectives require a minimum product life cycle of half a decade at which point the market and competitive parameters may be substantially different than they will be a scant two years hence, which your proposed guidelines ostensibly have been predicated upon. Extending readily apparent market trends leads one to an unalterable conclusion that a reduction in product size and weight substantially more aggressive than that recommended would represent a more prudent course of action. In consequence of this determination, or concurrence in the proposed guidelines regretfully must be withheld.

Whew! What did he say? The sentences are grammatically correct and the message is the same. But the tone is cumbersome, stilted, pompous. The message is unnecessarily obscured by the wordiness and choice of language. If anyone spoke this paragraph to you, your predictable reaction would be, "Is he putting me on?" Businessmen's files are full of such writing; certainly this extreme is much more prevalent than the former grammar school style. Readability can be enhanced with a more natural balance of short and long sentences, with more commonly used words, and less jargon:

> To be consistent with profit objectives, we believe the product guidelines should reflect market requirements five years away, rather than the two year reach used in your proposal. A five year criteria would result in a greater reduction in product size and weight than recommended, based on present trends. Therefore, we disagree with the proposed guidelines and recommend a more aggressive reduction.

A careful dissection of the three foregoing passages, which all communicate the same message, results in identifying several writing techniques that can be used to alter the tone effectively. Notice the difference in cadence or beat as you reread them. Notice also the differences in sentence structure — the similarity in structure of the first two and the variety in the last one. Notice the difference in choice of words. Notice also the more logical flow of the argument in the third example. Such considerations are a matter of writing style, which will be discussed in more detail in the next chapter. The objective should be, however, to achieve an overall tone that is conducive to easy readability.

Effective writing requires selecting an appropriate tone for the task at hand. The operative word here is *selecting*. To advance beyond average writing skills, the writer must understand this objective. He must realize that with or without conscious effort a tone will be established, and it is his responsibility to control it to maximum advantage. An honest respect for the audience is necessary, as well as a sensitivity to your own personality traits. A tone that retains the reader's interest is fundamental to achieving effectiveness. Likewise, natural readability will be more persuasive than a less natural, awkward tone. A wise person, with ambition to succeed, will not leave such matters to chance — particularly when the tools exist to manipulate the tone through his own writing skills.

9

FOR EFFECTIVE WRITING

TAILOR YOUR STYLE

BEAUTY IS in the eye of the beholder. Whoever first uttered those words (or perhaps they were initially exposed even in written form) had an intuitive grasp of *style*. It is reflected both in what was said, as well as the way in which it was said. Just as beauty has meaning only through individual interpretation, so does style. At the extreme, broad agreement can be reached as to what constitutes a "10" in the female (or male) form; or in "good style," whether it be in architecture, clothing, automotive design, or writing. But in the main, judgments regarding what is pleasing in style or beauty are very much a matter of personal taste.

The writing style of the expression, "Beauty is in the eye of the beholder," has enjoyed wide acceptance as attested to by its staying power. It would be difficult to identify, however, precisely why this is so. If the author had selected a different way to express the same thought, would it have achieved equal popularity? Of course, we will never know, but what if the saying had been:

- Each individual has his own standard of beauty.
- Everyone measures beauty against their own criteria.
- The beholder's eye determines what is beautiful.

None of these have the impact of the original, although each is grammatically correct and the message is clear. The difference is style. The original *sounds* better. The eight common words work naturally together to form a profound thought that is quickly grasped by all but the dullest of minds. It is difficult to convey to the beginning writer what style is and what it is not. It defies accurate description and yet all writers have an identifiable style. Principles of style for inexperienced writers to consider as they tailor their own style, which will be discovered in this chapter, are shown in Table 41.

Table 41

PRINCIPLES OF STYLE

- Reflect your natural personality
- Develop an ear for accepted grammar
- Maintain control
- Consider the rhythm
- Make the maximum use of vocabulary
- Learn to tailor the style to the circumstances
- Avoid obvious styling flaws

WRITE NATURALLY

More than any other single thing, *style* is a reflection of the personality holding the pen. If a writer is given sufficient exposure, a dominant style of writing will emerge. The style could be extremely precise and tightly organized. It could be laced with bits of humor, or consistently serious. It could reflect the statico of broken thoughts coming from a racing mind. It could reflect any of the many tones discussed in the previous chapter. It will surely reflect the intellect of the author through the variety, preciseness, and scope of the choice of words. It is futile to try to submerge your personality, for over a period of time your writing will give you away — and be more effective as a result.

On several occasions in this book, I have urged you to write as naturally as possible. Whatever is natural to you will be your style of writing. But how will you know what is *natural*? You will know by what writers refer to as your "ear." As you now know, all writing has a sound to it. If the rhythm and balance, if the flow of words, sound as though you could read them out loud comfortably, I would consider them to be natural to you.

But, what if your natural style is ineffective? Does that mean you are stuck with it? That you should accept your fate and look for another route up the ladder? Of course not. Style can be improved through study and effort. You were not born with an ingrained "ear" for writing. It was a developed skill. In some cases it was an accident of your education, your early environment, and your exposure, or lack of exposure, to good writing. This chapter will attempt to elucidate certain concepts of style that a beginning writer can work on to improve his own skill.

TRAIN YOUR EAR

As in every other facet of writing, style is conveyed through the fundamentals of accepted grammar. As we have seen, it is more than merely the use of correct grammar, but it certainly begins there. So the first element to check in tailoring your style is whether correct grammar sounds right to you. Conversely, if incorrect grammar sounds good to you, it is probably a source of your ineffectiveness. As we discussed, accepted grammar has a purpose — it results in the clear expression of thought. Therefore, adopting "correct" grammatical usage and construction can only improve your style. You can train your ear to accept and even prefer correct grammar through conscientious study of the subject and diligent practice. Keep it in the forefront of your consciousness. Examine your writing and the writing of others for mistakes. Read as much as you can. Given time, you will naturally adopt a style that avoids grammatical mistakes and the effectiveness of your writing will be enhanced.

MAINTAIN CONTROL

A weakness more prevalent than grammatical problems in the average writing style is the lack of control. Writing involves collecting a loosely interrelated series of thoughts that bounce around the writer's mind into an organized expression of the primary ideas he wants to communicate. To capture such free-thought on paper would be one style. This style, however, would hardly be conducive to persuasion or to clear understanding. To communicate effectively, the writer must sort through his thoughts, organize them, and control the reader's digestion of them. This control can be accomplished in a variety of ways, and it is just this difference in technique that separates one writer's style from another.

In a business environment, it is best to establish control with straightforward techniques. More sophisticated controls, such as "clues," *flashbacks, teasers*, and the like, are better left to mystery novelists and poets. The simple concepts presented in this book are powerful enough tools for most situations. The primary concepts that induce control are:

```
                        Table 42


            CONCEPTS THAT INDUCE CONTROL

            • Logical organization
            • Consistency and unity in
              sentences and paragraphs
            • Strategic emphasis
            • Parallel structure
            • Hooks
            • Format
```

Mastering these concepts, which were all discussed previously, and incorporating them into your writing will improve your control and evolve into a more effective style. In particular, the intelligent use of *parallel structure* and *effective hooks* will give your writing instant style. Chapters 5 and 6 discussed these concepts in some detail. To move forward in your writing skill, to really stand out among your peers, you should develop your ear for effective hooks. In the haste of writing, many people ignore hooks entirely and the reader is left to grope his own way through the letter. Others use the same hook (forms *however, but, accordingly, in summary*) over and over again, such that the mere repetition reduces their effectiveness. It is better to vary the hooks and even occasionally avoid a direct, obvious hook in favor of a more subtle one that causes the reader to consider a point from a different angle. A more readable style will incorporate a full range of hook techniques. This is more work for the author, but the reader will benefit without ever being aware of it. The writing will become more readable, more comprehensible, and more persuasive as a result.

An obvious stylistic consideration is the use of formatting techniques. The format that an author (or organization) prefers will become as much a fingerprint of his style as anything else. When tailoring your own style, it might be wise initially to emulate the format of those whom you consider to be successful. As we discussed previously, it may be self-defeating to be overly creative or original in the use of new formats. Until you have a well established reputation, it is better to use accepted techniques. But that still leaves considerable flexibility in choosing a format style for the task at hand. Effective writing requires that the format support the overall effort, and a rigid style, followed without deviation, probably lacks the flexibility to be effective in every circumstance.

CONSIDER THE RHYTHM

A more individualistic style characteristic is the rhythm of your writing. Rhythm is transmitted somewhat through the choice of words, but more prominently in the use of punctuation and sentence structure. Commas, semicolons, and periods all call for pauses of varying degrees. As discussed in a previous chapter, simple sentences have a different rhythm than compound sentences, or compound-complex sentences. The use of prepositional phrases, expanded verbs, parenthetical expressions, and verbals all result in a different cadence and rhythm to the words.

You can tailor your style by being conscious of the rhythm of your writing. Reread it to yourself, out loud if you must, as though you were speaking at the podium . Are any phrases awkward to your ear? Do you stumble here and there? Do you find yourself trying to read two short sentences as though they were one? Or pausing in the middle of a long sentence as though you were separating it into two sentences? Such rhythm considerations can be controlled by you. Rewrite if necessary until the rhythm sounds more natural to you. Stop when it does, and the result will reflect your ear, your style.

Some general thoughts relative to rhythm may be helpful for a beginning writer. First, oral communications have variety. A more natural writing rhythm would also exhibit variety. A long string of simple sentences should be avoided. Likewise, repetitive use of expanded verbs (the river ran *in a torrent of foamy spray* over the precipice) or expanded nouns (the river, *wide and tranquil at this point*, meandered out of sight) become laborious to read. A paragraph that has more variety of rhythm from one sentence to the next will likely be more natural.

Variety in the use of loose or periodic sentence structure will also improve writing style. A *loose* sentence is one that expresses a basic thought followed by an open ended amplification of the thought that can extend as long as the author chooses:

> The production order was running late, but the promised timing could be met through adding a second shift for a week.

A *periodic* sentence, on the other hand, is one that interrupts the basic thought by inserting additional information in the middle of the sentence:

> The order, through no fault of the plant manager,
> was running late.

Each form, loose and periodic, has a different rhythm. A conscientious writer will develop an ear that is sensitive to this difference and strive to incorporate a natural variety into his work.

A final tip on rhythm is to look for balance. Just as a non-symetrical shape is an awkward style except in the hands of the most gifted artists, an unbalanced sentence can be awkward to the ear. This is particularly noticeable when using *correlative expressions* (not only, but also). Good style dictates that the grammatical form following correlative expressions be in balance by having a similar rhythm:

> The new book is not only *more complete*, but also
> *more difficult*.

Watch for this when encountering comparisons, positive/negative sections, or other related connectives such as:

- Not only — — but also
- Both — — and
- Either — — or
- Neither — — nor
- Does not — — it does
- First — — second — — third

If balance can be achieved in the phrases following such correlative expressions, your style will be more acceptable because it will be unoffensive to the "inner ear" of the average reader.

STYLE THROUGH VOCABULARY

Up to this point we have seen that a certain style can be mechanically developed by considering the correct use of fundamentals, by using control techniques, by planning the format, and by establishing a natural rhythm. The last general tool at the writer's command to tailor his own style is his vocabulary, or semantics — the selection of the specific words the writer uses to express his thoughts. Your style will reflect the richness or paucity of your vocabulary, and the effectiveness of your style will be enhanced or reduced accordingly. As we have said repeatedly, it is unnecessary to force long words into your writing to appear smart; in fact, it is more effective (and more difficult) to find the simplest word possible that accurately connotes the intended idea. But the more color, the more life, the more preciseness you can induce into your writing through variety in your choice of words, the more effective your style will become.

In a business situation, the jargon of the office will frequently creep into your vocabulary. Used properly, this is not in itself bad. Companies may utilize certain phrases that when widely understood can be useful to conserve words, without sacrificing a clear understanding. To a certain audience, it may be appropriate to write, "We need to *put this stake in the ground* as soon as possible." It may be a more effective style than an explicit explanation of a "need to firmly establish a point as a basic criteria or assumption in order to eliminate it from further consideration as a variable." Such simplifying jargon definitely has a place in good style. But the author must carefully consider the needs of the audience before resorting to such jargon.

STYLE ADAPTATION

Another facet of tailoring your style that may need to be considered in a business environment is *whose* style your writing should reflect. If you are a novelist, you have the freedom to present solely your own unique, preferred style. If you are high enough up the ladder in business, you may also enjoy this luxury. But more typically, your writing must reflect an accepted style of your company, your organization within the company, or perhaps your boss (particularly if he will be signing what you are writing). Such writing assignments are among the most difficult, and most frequently encountered. The author must submerge his natural style and affect the style of another. He must frequently be a camelion to adopt a satisfactory style for one purpose one day, another the next, and another the next. This challenge can be met, however, through a good understanding of the tools that establish a "style," as discussed in this chapter. The skill of being able to adapt a writing style to the circumstances stands out among those who progress up the ladder.

RECOGNIZING POOR STYLE

The foregoing has been an attempt to clarify the nebulous concept of good writing style. It is also useful to know what good style is not. Few hard rules can be given in this area, because after all, "Beauty is in the eye of the beholder." But, through personal experience and through reading the advice of others, certain prominent stylistic flaws can be identified. In business writing, it is wise to avoid the following:

First Person: It is usually superfluous to insert the first person into business correspondence. The "I believe," "we consider," and "in our opinion" phrases seldom add to the content of the idea to be expressed and may detract. It is more effective to state the thought positively — identification of whose thought it was is usually clear anyway.

Inventing Words: It is tempting and widespread in business to manufacture new words by adding the insidious suffixes "-wise," "-ism," "-ize," "-ful," "-ly," or the prefixes "non-," "de-," "dis-," and "anti-." I refer you to Edwin Newman's *A Civil Tongue* for more on the subject. To maximize your effectiveness stylewise, non-insertion of jargonisms is advisedly recommended.

Type of Habit: *Type* is a useless adjective (this *type of style* . . .). It's use can always be avoided and the style improved without this trite expression.

Manner and Nature: When used, the resultant phrases always sound stilted or pompous. (In the manner of . . . , or comprehensive in nature . . .) If your ear prefers such usage, force yourself to draw a line through it and ask yourself if anything has been lost.

Trite Expressions: Although somewhat more difficult to spot, because what may be *trite* to one person may seem fresh to another, be on guard for over-worn expressions (the acid test . . . , . . . up to the bitter end.) They are not really wrong, but they lack impact because of their overuse.

Foreign Language: Very few foreign language expressions are widely enough known to use safely in business correspondence. It is best to avoid the temptation entirely. But, if you cannot resist, be sure you use it in the right context. Do not use "de facto" for "de jure" inadvertently. If you want to cite a sense of *deja vu*, be sure it adds to the effectiveness of your message.

Poetic Writing: Alliterations, flowery prose, ornate writing or other poetic overwriting seem out of place in normal business correspondence. It is better to use standard words and phrases — more than enough are available to express every nuance of thought without resorting to sophomoric gimmicks.

Unpleasant Combinations: The sound of the words when combined should not result in tongue twisters (some people shun the seashore).

Dialectal Words: In particular, avoid vulgar words, swearing, crude words *(gut feel)*, illiteracies *(ain't)* and colliquial phrases *(down the road a piece)*. Your style should reflect a positive image of yourself and such grammar is not widely acclaimed.

Slang and Jargon: What may sound natural to you in your normal conversation, may distract or confuse the reader unless he has a comparable background. Rather than take a chance, it is safer to use standard words. In addition, much slang is tasteless *(lousy, slob, rap)* and at a minimum reflects a weak vocabulary. Jargon also may naturally enter your writing. Jargon, particularly business jargon, however, may be meaningless outside of the special field that originates the work.

Technical Words: Unless your writing is directed toward a very select group that you know will comprehend the technical words, your style would be more effective if ideas are translated into their simplest form for the reader. It is best to avoid calling a cherry tree a *Prunus Rosaceae*, or a calf muscle the *gastrocnemius*, unless some specific technical point is being made. The objective should always be to clearly communicate to the reader, not to artificially impress him.

Having been exposed to the foregoing concepts of good style and poor style, it would be instructive for you to compare several of your most recent letters or papers against these suggestions. Look particularly for similarities in the different pieces of writing. Can you find your style? Do you see any of the common flaws covered in this chapter? If not, you are indeed an advanced writer of some skill and your style may need little tailoring. If you do (and most people will), try rewriting certain passages to improve the style. Rewrite until it has a natural sound to you. This is a cumbersome process and most active businessmen will object to the struggle. Nevertheless, if you are earnest in wanting to tailor your style for more effective writing, no better way exists to do it.

Initially you will find many flaws, and the reconstruction will require strenuous thought. Very soon, however, you will spot such flaws as you write and avoid them before you finish writing. If you sensitize your ear to proper grammar, good balance, natural rhythm, and continuity of control, your style will become effortless. When you reach this point, the chances are that you will be recognized in your business circles as a "good writer," and the evidence will be in the power of your pen — the objectives of clearly and persuasively presenting your thoughts will be achieved.

10

FOR EFFECTIVE WRITING

WRITE EFFICIENTLY

A MAJOR impediment to effective communication is the tendency to be too wordy — for saying more than is necessary to clearly make a point. To write *efficiently*, to be concise and precise, is an important objective for improving the effectiveness of your writing. Clarity can be sacrificed if the writer becomes carried away with the temptation to be verbose. If the message becomes rambling and disorganized because the writer is attempting to say too much, the reader may "go fishing" — he may start casting his eyes about in the hopes of striking the key point. The more that is written, the more difficult it is to achieve the other objectives of organization, emphasis, control and tone. Experience gives a writer an appreciation of how important it is to write efficiently, and how easily this objective can be lost unless it is practiced religiously. Principles of achieving writing efficiency are shown in Table 43.

Table 43

PRINCIPLES FOR EFFICIENCY

- Control the egotistical urge to impress the reader.
- Avoid emulating jargonistic writing.
- Avoid rationalizing over-writing for business reasons.
- Edit thoroughly to improve clarity.
- Simplify with good organization.
- Simplify with sound grammar fundamentals.
- Simplify with good vocabulary.
- Avoid the 10 most common flaws.

Writing efficiently goes against many deep seated aspects of human nature. It is natural for all of us to try to impress those around us with our knowledge, our wisdom, our insightfulness, our perception, and our other self-granted attributes. This is particularly tempting when addressing a captive audience, or at least one that cannot interrupt you, such as the eventual readers of an author's work. This may be prevalent in the business world, where impressing those around you is the name of the game. It takes a high degree of self-discipline to control the urge to write all you know about a subject, rather than focusing on the more relevant material only. It is also difficult to avoid using the most extravagent language at your command rather than saying the same thing simply and directly.

A great deal of the jargon encountered in business correspondence (the corporateeze we are all familiar with) can be attributed to another aspect of human nature. That is — the tendency to emulate those who are considered to be successful. The jargon of superiors, or commonly in use throughout a company for that matter, will frequently be adopted by beginning writers. They will reduce their use of familiar phrases and sentence structure they may have used for years in school, and begin to absorb new ways of expressing themselves into their writing. In some respects, this is healthy. It is conducive to effective communication to use words and phrases your readers will readily understand. But, on the other hand, the copying of popular jargon does perpetuate the use of bad writing practices as well — particularly the unnecessary words and windy phrases so commonly utilized.

In addition to human nature fighting simple writing, many aspects of the business environment also tend to promote extensive writing. In a business context, the writer may feel compelled to cover a subject in more depth than is necessary, or use more words than necessary, under the misguided conception that the message will be more accurate. Much business writing appears to strain for exactness, for legalistic terminology, intending to be absolutely clear. Often, however, such language can only be interpreted by the courts.

In business, it is frequently necessary to qualify the content of the communication, which may also lead to additional wordiness. Positions taken have to be placed in the context of certain background information. Recommendations are made in the context of certain assumptions being valid. Data presented are identified as to source and timeliness. The typical businessman is well trained to protect himself at all times, and the many qualifiers in the forefront of his thinking finds their way into his writing.

Another impediment to simple writing arising from the influence of a business orientation is the desire to cover all the angles. A smart businessman, particularly one with an ambition to get ahead, makes sure he has examined every side of an issue, has considered all possibilities, has recognized every alternative, and has addressed all possible questions. This mentality is a major source of the overwriting frequently encountered in business correspondence. The writer does not want to take the risk that the reader will think something has been overlooked.

Overwriting is frequently a matter of insecurity on the part of the author. He is not certain of his subject or the necessary qualifications or the related issues that are relevant. He may also be uncertain about his audience — are they more knowledgeable, or less? will they be more, or less, critical? more receptive, or require convincing? A writer that is overly concerned about such matters will find it difficult to focus succinctly on his own ideas.

In business, time is money. Businessmen do not appreciate receiving long-winded communications. It is more than a matter of convenience to some; they simply lack the time to read everything they recieve. Much of their correspondence is even handled on the run during the day within a few mintues stolen between long meetings. A concise, well written piece in those circumstances is worth its weight in gold. An overly thorough, completely comprehensive discussion paper seldom earns respect for the author — and seldom is read in its entirety.

As we have encountered elsewhere in this book, clarity is the overriding objective for written communications. Of course, it is possible to be brief to a fault and lose clarity. It takes deliberate mental effort to balance the requirements of saying enough, without being too wordy. Business judgment and training are essential to know where to draw the line. In practice, it requires writing naturally and then rereading your draft to edit any superfluous sentences or words. To simplify, it may even take wholesale rewriting of major passages. The more the discipline of editing your own work is followed, the more your original drafts will begin to reflect sound writing skills and the efficient use of words.

Judgment and practice can be supplemented with knowledge of certain fundamental writing concepts that are conducive to concise writing. In addition, numerous flaws in average correspondence can be identified that will help the beginning writer avoid the same mistakes. This chapter will attempt to summarize the key fundamentals to follow and the most obvious flaws to avoid for more efficient writing.

FUNDAMENTALS FOR EFFICIENCY

Two fundamental areas of writing techniques, whose mastery will facilitate efficient writing, are the concepts of *effective organization* and, secondly, the actual *construction* of the sentences using words most effectively. The first deals with an efficient ordering of the thought process; the second with an efficient presentation of those thoughts.

Section II of this book was devoted to discussing the three broad writing objectives that give organization to written communications. The concept of focusing the content of your writing directly relates to efficient writing. The objective should be to stick to the point; learn to be self-critical and avoid the temptation to wander off the subject. Having written a splendidly constructed paragraph or sentence, with perfect selection of words to exactly express the desired thought, it is a heartrendering effort to draw a line through it. It is a common mistake to fall in love with your own prose; it becomes a piece of your mind that you wish to expose to the world. Be on guard for this self-protecting tendency and concentrate on the primary writing objectives. If the thought does not add to the effectiveness of the communication, if it does not focus on the intended content, forget it — the world can do well without it.

Of course, the more logical the organization of the writing, the more likely it is that the writing will be kept as concise as possible. Many words are wasted trying to straighten out poor organization. Whenever you catch yourself restating an argument, or rephrasing the same thought a different way, or looping back to pick up a previous line of thought, or referring to something to be addressed later, or using complicated transitional ideas, you should look for ways to reorganize your work to avoid the extra words.

The organizational value of good formatting techniques can also greatly assist in trimming words from a communication. A well placed heading can serve the place of several transition sentences. A parenthetical statement interjected at an appropriate spot can replace a separate paragraph. A list of key points can greatly simplify the presentation of them as well as give emphasis to their relationship. The "slide" format for a long report is an invaluable tool to reduce superfluous writing. Although the primary objective of formatting considerations is to establish control, many of the techniques will have the secondary benefit of writing more efficiently.

In addition to careful organization, certain fundamentals of grammar and writing style are conducive to using words efficiently. First, basic sentence structure can assist or defeat this objective. Prepositional phrases can be used to frequently avoid the need for an additional sentence. An appositive (George Washington, *the first President*, . . .)is also a simplifying technique. Non-restrictive clauses, on the other hand, complicate a sentence — sometimes unnecessarily. Another particularly troublesome structure is the negative-positive statement:

> The answer is not to give up, but rather to fight harder.

versus

> The answer is to fight harder.

Another grammatical choice that will normally eliminate unnecessary words (and have other benefits as well) is to replace passive verbs with active verbs. Try it for yourself. In virtually every instance you can save a couple of words.

USE EFFICIENT WORDS

A more difficult thing to train yourself to do in order to save words is to use better words to begin with. This is difficult because you write with perhaps 10% or less of your actual vocabulary. As you write, you use the words that pop into your head and press on. You end up constructing sentences and all the rest based on the nouns and verbs that occur to you as you write. In general, the inexperienced writer relies too heavily on adjectives and adverbs to give clarity to weak, general nouns and verbs. It is much more effective, more persuasive, more clear, and certainly less wordy to utilize more descriptive and accurate nouns and verbs in the first place. The only way to train yourself to do this is to force yourself to take the time to search for the right word. Get to know "Mr. Thesaurus" intimately. When you read a phrase that impresses you, jot it down for future use in your own writing. Give yourself a challenge in each new letter to try a word you do not commonly use. The emphasis, naturally should be on clarity and consiseness, not on adornment or pomposity. But, such constant self-reminders to consider stronger words will lead to strengthening your vocabulary, and more importantly, to expanding the use of your full vocabulary from the 10% range to 50% or more with little additional effort. Your writing will not only be more concise, but probably many of the other writing objectives will be enhanced as well.

We previously discussed the advantages and disadvantages of the use of *figures of speech*, many of which make up the jargon so roundly criticized in business communications. A distinction needs to be made, however, between the proper use of jargon that can promote simplified writing and the verbose jargon that is the target of the writing critics. The latter can be identified by the length of the sentences (25 words or more), the number of letters per word (15 or over), the familiar word endings (-wise, -eze, -ism), and the convoluted flow of reasoning. On the other hand, the simplifying jargon, which also smacks of corporateeze language, may have a rightful place in effective correspondence. Phrases such as "cost-to-trade," "roll-back of prices," "distressed pricing" and comparable market jargon can save many explanatory words when used in business circles familiar with the phrases. Every business discipline has their own technical jargon that becomes indispensible to effective communications. Less technical jargon such as "thought starters," "real world results," "stake-in-the-ground," "sound footing," and the like are also invaluable word savers. When used intelligently, jargon can be conducive to writing efficiently. The key to its effective use, however, is in knowing your audience — if you are certain the phrases that are very familiar to you will be as readily accepted by your intended audience, they can (and probably should) be used for ease of communication.

One fundamental that can effectively reduce unnecessary words if used with skill is the use of *pronoun reference*. In an earlier chapter we discussed the risk of misusing pronouns and losing control. But, when used correctly they can greatly simplify writing. Rather than useless repetition of the nouns or ideas being used for the antecedent, a well placed pronoun can be just as clear and avoid the wordiness. The major caution in this regard is when using general pronouns (*this, it, they*, etc.) that you double check to be certain the reference is clear and can be interpreted only one way. Ambiguous pronoun references may lead to even using additional words to straighten out the confusion, thus defeating the purpose of the sample pronoun.

10 COMMON FLAWS

Being aware of the foregoing concepts of good organization and fundamentals of good grammar will prevent the bulk of overwriting tendencies. In addition, it may be helpful to consider ten common flaws that are frequently encountered in average writing, which contribute to unnecessary words. An occasional check of your own writing against this list would be enlightening.

1. The use of passive voice should be reserved solely for instances in which the subject clearly is intended to be acted upon. An active verb is always a more direct way to express an idea.

2. Avoid using *there*. It will always add unnecessary words to a sentence. It is a frequent, lazy way to avoid the use of an active, precise verb that could make the sentence more effective. Its primary uses are (1) to mean a location (. . . over there), and better ways usually exist to express even this thought, or (2) as an interjection to express satisfaction or approval (There!). It is ineffective as the subject of a sentence (There are . . .).

3. Avoid windy phrases for which a perfectly good word can be substituted.

In a careful manner	Carefully
At the present time	Now
In the event of	If
In the majority of cases	Usually
In consideration of	Considering
In relation to	With
This type of thing is	This is

4. Never use the phrase, "In other words, . . ." This is a clear signal that more efficient writing can be utilized. Even if you are compelled to rephrase an idea, it is unnecessary to introduce the fact that you are doing so. It is better, however, to avoid the restatement entirely — express what you mean clearly and succiently the first time.

5. Avoid worthless qualifiers such as *very, little, about, much, some, pretty*, or *rather*. These words at best are vague softeners that most people ignore, and at worst are ambiguous and beg for additional clarifying words. If any qualification is necessary, use an accurate phrase.

6. Edit out all redundencies that creep into figures of speech almost unnoticed, such as "advanced forward," "inside of," "small in size," or "absolutely certain."

7. Eliminate unnecessary introductions such as "In my opinion, . . . ," "The reason why . . . ," "One of the most . . . ," "As a matter of fact . . . ," "In fact . . . ," "The fact is . . . ," "Undoubtedly . . . ," or Obviously . . ." Not only are such introductions unnecessary, they are immediately suspect. Something that is obvious or a fact probably does not need the lable. Further, to announce something based on your opinion suggests alternative views exist and immediately weakens the point.

8. Watch out for overstating the case with unnecessary emphasis, using words such as *mandatory, paramount importance, crucial to success, maximum, optimum*, or *critical*. These are usually exaggerations that can be eliminated without reducing effectiveness. Save them for situations that truly are critical and the emphasis will be even more emphatic.

9. Use the positive form whenever possible, rather than the negative; it is normally shorter and also more emphatic.

It is not dissimilar	It is similar
Did not remember	Forgot
Did not pay attention to	Ignored
Did not have confidence in	Distrusted
It is not a bad idea to	It is a good idea to

10. Avoid needless repetition of a word or phrase by proper use of pronoun reference, by effective organization, and by other techniques such as the use of acronyms (NAACP). While an effective way to simplify writing without losing meaning, avoiding repetition must be done carefully. Pronoun references must be clearly tied to only one antecedent. Acronyms must be well known by your audience (or the words spelled out, at least the first time they are used in the text).

The objective of writing efficiently is the final consideration in achieving a more persuasive writing style. The concepts of clarity and strategic emphasis are enhanced by more precise writing. Tone and style objectives are also compatible with more focused, concise writing. Of course, by editing over-zealously, it is possible to reduce effectiveness in these areas. But, as in most skills, it becomes a matter of experience and judgment. Your ear will tell you when you have gone too far — just as it should warn you when you become too verbose. The challenge is to achieve all of the nine objectives outlined in this book simultaneously for maximum effectiveness. They are all interrelated and all impact on the overall effectiveness of the final work. If you can keep these objectives in the forefront of your thinking, if you incorporate these concepts routinely into your writing, if you develop the ear to write naturally without violating these objectives, your writing will become a major asset in your climb up the ladder.

SECTION FOUR

MAKE EFFECTIVE WRITING

A HABIT

11

MAKE EFFECTIVE WRITING A HABIT

EXECUTIVES everywhere are painfully aware of the scarcity of skilled writers — both in their own organizations, as well as among those they deal with daily. The value of writing skill to up and coming men and women in business cannot be exaggerated. Their ideas will gain more merit from the effective way they are presented in writing, and also their very skill at communicating their thoughts and other matters will gain recognition from their superiors. The unusual persuasiveness of their writing will enhance the attainment of the underlying business objectives of their communications. Their reputation for being "good writers" will be a positive asset in assuring their success in climbing the ladder.

Those with the intelligence and drive to succeed in the other areas of competition for business success, surely are astute enough to comprehend, learn and use the fundamental concepts of effective writing. The missing ingredients for the multitude of people who have not mastered writing skills, even though they are successful in all other respects, seem to be:

- A recognition that their writing style plays a major part in their career success, and
- An understanding of the writing objectives that are conducive to effective communications and how best to achieve such objectives.

Whether a person is about to launch a career, or has been groping up the ladder for 10 or 15 years, it is invaluable to assess your own writing style and critically evaluate if it is an asset or a weakness. The foregoing chapters present a reasonable framework to make such an evaluation. Your recent communications could be reviewed against the criteria for effective communications in each chapter. Furthermore, the letters and written material of others, particularly those individuals you admire and consider to be successful, could also be reviewed in this manner. I predict that with suprisingly little effort you will be able to make improvements on virtually everything you pick up.

The secret to mastering the art of writing is to make good writing habitual. Habitual in the sense that your original draft comes closer to a high standard, and habitual in the way you approach polishing the work before you are satisfied it is final. Just as you can educate yourself in the fundamentals of effective writing, you can train yourself to adopt good writing habits. This chapter offers my 10 commandments for achieving this end.

Table 44

10 COMMANDMENTS FOR GOOD WRITING HABITS

1. Study the fundamentals
2. Get organized before you start
3. Reread everything you write
4. Rewrite until it sounds right
5. Edit constructively, but ruthlessly
6. Project yourself into the audience
7. Read extensively for business and pleasure
8. Borrow shamelessly from good writers
9. Practice good writing at every opportunity
10. Strive for perfection

---

1. Study The Fundamentals

Good writing fundamentals go beyond the essential objective of using accepted grammar. They encompass the three basic objectives of good organization — to focus the content, to plan the format, and to orchestrate the logic; and also the five objectives for persuasive writing — clarity, emphasis, tone, style and efficiency. A high caliber of writing skill may be achieved through conscientious study and application of these fundamentals. To sustain a high level of skill, however, such study cannot be confined to a once-in-a-lifetime experience, such as most people employ. It is insufficient to have received straight A's in all of your English courses in school. To sustain your skill, the study of writing fundamentals must be adopted as a lifelong hobby. Good writers constantly refresh their memory on the fundamentals, through frequent use of reference books, dictionaries, Thesaurus books, and other writing manuals.

2. Get Organized Before You Start

Make it a habit to plan what you want to write before you begin the first sentence. Prepare an outline that includes the points you want to cover, focuses and logically organizes the content, and serves as a roadmap for your writing. The outline may only exist in your head, but the step is indispensible for effective writing. The complexity and detail of the outline could vary from scribbled notes to an elaborate, formal outline, depending on the nature of the communication and the time available. Collect the necessary backup and support-material to have on hand as you write. Organize your thoughts, including jotting down key phrases you want to use. Carefully consider your audience as well during the organizational process. This habit will not be time consuming — to the contrary, it invariably saves time in the end and is key to becoming a good writer.

3. Reread Everything You Write

Even the most skilled writers must polish their work before the various objectives of good writing can be met. You can bet that those with consistently high standards of performance have developed this habit. In business, some of the worst writing eminates from smart men who egotistically dictate everything they "write" and leave it to their secretaries to "get it out" in their absence. They pride themselves in never having to change a word. Even the most brilliant people I know cannot consistently produce good work using this method. Not only is rereading your writing a good habit, it is even better to do it twice — the first time for a check on the broad objectives of style, tone, logic, format and focus; the second reading, as slow and meticulously as necessary, to reconsider word selection, sentence structure, spelling, and other fundamentals. This only sounds laborious to those who have not developed this sound writing habit.

4. Rewrite Until It Sounds Right

It is a mistake to become attached to your original draft — seldom is it the best that you can do. In addition, you can be your own best critic. Develop the habit of expecting to make changes. If you dictate, train your secretary to expect some modifications. If you write long-hand, consider using legal pads with plenty of room to make corrections, or write your draft double spaced so you can easily insert or change things. Trust your ear and your judgment, and do not hesitate to rewrite major portions if necessary. It is easy to become mentally lazy and accept inferior work; make it as convenient as possible for yourself to rewrite until it sounds right.

5. Edit Constructively, But Ruthlessly

Just as rewriting requires the proper attitude to abandon your original product, editing requires an even firmer mental toughness. Be ruthless with your original efforts and eliminate every word that is unnecessary, every phrase that can be simplified, and every sentence or paragraph that is irrelevant. Efficient writing is more effective. When in doubt, leave it out. It is better to err on the side of simplicity. However, "simple" writing is not necessarily simple to achieve. It requires clear, concise thinking to produce clear, concise writing and the discipline of one process reinforces the other.

6. Project Yourself Into The Audience

Novelists may write for themselves; businessmen write for an audience. Frequently, books on writing style urge that the authors should write to please themselves, and by so doing presumably will have a better chance to please whatever audience their books encounter. Business writing is generally much more focused — to a specific audience and with a well defined business purpose. Skillful business writers have an ability to project themselves into their intended audience; they can anticipate their audience's needs and focus on how best to inform and persuade them. It is a good habit to consider how your audience will react to your words: How will they read your work (remember the approach discussed in the chapter on formats)? Is their background compatible with the depth and scope of coverage of the material? Is the tone conducive to constructive communications? Will they follow your train of thought? If you were them, what would you think of your writing? Habitually asking yourself such questions as you are rereading your first draft will frequently lead to changes that can make your final work more effective.

7. Read Extensively For Business And Pleasure

The best advice that can be given to people aspiring to improve their writing is to read extensively. Reading is to the mind what exercise is to the body. The elusive writing "ear" can be trained by reading another's writing. Care must be taken, of course, to be selective in the material you read; concentrate on respected periodicals (*Forbes*, *Fortune*, *The Wall Street Journal*, and the like), read the books of respected authors (in any field, not only business), and be particularly sensitive to the writing style of those you respect in your business circles. Being well read will greatly improve your vocabulary, as well as your style. Be alert for particularly effective phrases or styles of expressing an idea that impress you. It is a good idea to start a collection of words or phrases that you would like to use in your own writing — underline something that you like and throw it in a folder for future reference. The more you read, the more your own writing ear will be honed and sensitized to the sound of good writing style.

8. Borrow Shamelessly From Good Writers

This habit is particularly useful for neophytes in the business world, but has suprisingly strong implications throughout your career. In the first year or two after joining a new company, or for the first several months after joining a new organization within the company, it is wise to adopt the best of the writing style and particular jargon in use at the time. Being aware of sound writing objectives, you should be able to select the wheat from the chaff and not copy someone else's bad habits. It is more effective to use phrases or jargon commonly used in your business circles, than to stubbornly impose your own natural style on the "system." Your audience will be more receptive and their rapid comprehension will be facilitated by using terminology and formats they are accustomed to reading. In addition, to the extent that you use good judgment in borrowing only the best, your "natural" style will be improved by absorbing the good habits of others.

9. Practice Good Writing At Every Opportunity

The more you write, the better your writing will become — if you practice meeting the objectives of effective writing on every occasion. The sound advice, attributed to Vince Lombardi, that, "Practice doesn't make perfect; perfect practice makes perfect," is as true for writing, as it is for football. If you allow sloppy writing to be published, poor habits will sneak into your work. It takes a continual effort and constant diligence to enforce good writing habits. It also takes experience, which can only be gained through the act of composing. Actively seek out assignments that will challenge your writing skill; most of your peers will avoid them.

Table 44

10 COMMANDMENTS FOR GOOD WRITING HABITS

1. Study the fundamentals
2. Get organized before you start
3. Reread everything you write
4. Rewrite until it sounds right
5. Edit constructively, but ruthlessly
6. Project yourself into the audience
7. Read extensively for business and pleasure
8. Borrow shamelessly from good writers
9. Practice good writing at every opportunity
10. Strive for perfection

Offer to draft letters for your boss. Put your oral recommendations in writing. Write memos to the file for future reference. Write, write, write whenever you can. But whatever you write, make it right!

10. Strive For Perfection

The primary target audience for this book, those with an ambition to climb the ladder of success, probably already have developed this habit. But it remains a mystery to me why so many who are perfectionists in many other respects remain complacent regarding their writing habits. Many successful executives, for example, rely heavily on their secretaries to correct spelling and grammatical errors, openly joking about their shortcomings. They seem to regard it as demeaning to clutter their minds with such trivia. Their thought processes are reserved for truly significant matters. For consistent, effective writing, however, such expediencies should be avoided. Press yourself, and those writing for you if that is the case, for perfection. Several of the foregoing habits can only be developed through this best, most important habit.

Armed with the knowledge of how to achieve the objectives of effective writing and with the carefully cultivated habits for applying such knowledge, you are well prepared to assault the ladder. Your writing skill will be an important asset to separate you from the crowd. The recognition you will earn for being a "good writer" will be invaluable to your career progress. You will find your superiors relying on your writing skills, as much as your professional advice in your field. You will find your communications being more effective in fulfilling your business objectives. The more you perfect such skills, the more natural it will become; so that all of the hard work it initially took to achieve effective writing will eventually become effortless. Having achieved such a skill, protect it as a personal treasure; it will serve you well as you write your way up the ladder.

INDEX

Acronyms, proper use 103
Active verbs, to save words 141
Active voice, verbs 39, 109
Adaptation, in style 131
Adjectives, use 15
Adverbs, use 15
Agreement, in number 37
Affect, effect, usage 42
Antecedent, of pronouns 41
Antidotes, use of 58
Agreement, psychology of 83, 84
Arguments, declaring writer's
  position 59, 83
Articles, leaving out, what they are 17
Attitude, effects tone 120
Audience, consider in focusing ... 56

Balance, for style 130
Borrow, from good writers 151
Business correspondence unique ... 5
Business environment
  demands 3
  causes wordiness 136
Business letter, format 70

Clarity
  faulty parallelism 97
  faulty pronoun reference 96
  goal of grammar fundamentals . 27
  jargon use and misuse 101
  misplaced modifiers 97
  thru simplicity 137
  use of fundamentals 103
Clauses
  independent 23
  subordinate 22
  what they are 23
Coherence, of paragraphs 86
Colloquial words 43
Colon (:), use of 31
Commas, use of 33
Comparisons
  for adjectives and adverbs 39
  make complete 39
Complex sentence 25
Compound
  predicates 16
  sentence 25
  subjects 16

Compound-complex sentence 25
Concrete, verbs 112
Conjugations, for verbs 37
Conjunctions
  use 15
  coordinating 15
  subordinating 15
Conjunctive adverbs, use 15
Connections, standard hooks 87
Connotation, of words 99
Consiseness, thru logic 138
Consistency, of paragraphs 86
Control
  an element of style 127
  through format 66
  through logical grouping 81
  through paragraphs and
  sentences 67
  through punctuation 67
Counterbalance, weights of an
  argument 84

Dangling modifiers 46
Dashes, for punctuation 33
Declensions for words and
  pronouns 37
Dennotation, of words 99
Dialetic words 133
Dictionary, importance of 29

Ear
  natural 126
  training of.................. 12
  through reading 150
  what it is 12, 128
Editing 150
Effectiveness, in writing 53
Effective organization, objectives .. 4
Emphasis
  control of................... 107
  importance of 107
  through formatting 115
  through sentence structure ... 113
  through choice of verbs 109
Essay, format 72
Exaggerations, avoid 142
Exclamation mark (!), use of 31
Executive summary 76
                                    (continued)

155

Expanded nouns 129
Expanded verbs 129

Figures of speech
    what they are 100
    saves words 140
First person 132
"First-degree" words, for clarity .. 99
Focus
    expanding the content 59
    planning the depth 58
    planning the scope 57
    question relevancy 59
    recognizing the audience 56
    what it is 55
For, at end of sentence for
    emphasis 114
Foreign language 133
Format
    achieving control 66
    alternative methods 69
    consider attachments 76
    executive summary 76
    for style 128
    importance of 64
    what it is 63
Formatting, save words 138
Formatting techniques, objectives
    of 66
Funneling down, logic concept ... 82

Gerunds, use 19
Grammar
    definition 11
    fetishes 9
    in transition 11
    importance of fundamentals ... 10
    use a reference book 34
Grammatically correct 11
Grouping, logical concepts 81

Habits, for good writing 148
Hooks
    for style 128
    what they are 87
Human nature, an enemy of
    efficiency 136

Idioms, proper use 102
"In other words," avoid 142

Incomplete comparisons 39
Infinitives
    use of 21
    tense of 21
Inflections, what they are 35
Insecurity, causes wordiness 137
Interest, how to establish 120
Inventing words 132

Jargon
    can save words 140
    in business 101
    in style 133
    what it is 101
    wordiness 136

Location, key to emphasis 108
Logic
    conveyed through grammar 86
    psychology of argument 83
    use of hooks 87
Logical groupings 81
Logical completeness 88
Loose sentence structure 129

Management presence 3
Mannerisms 132
Memo, format 71
Metaphor 100

Natural ear, in style 126
"Nature" habit 132
Non-restrictive clauses and
    phrases 32
"Not," how to avoid 113
Nouns 13

Object, of sentence 13
Objectives, in writing 53
Omission, errors of 45
Opinion, use of 109
Order, of paragraphs 86
Organization
    aids efficiency 138
    logical 80
Overstatement, in emphasis 109
Outline
    helps focus 60
    necessary preparation 55

(continued)

Outline   (continued)
  plan the logic 80
  use of 55

Paperwork, an archaic medium .. 62
Paragraph, "good" characteristics 86
Parallel structure
  concept 47
  for clarity 97
Parenthesis, use of 33
Participles
  use of 19
  tense of 19
Parts of speech 12
Passive voice, when to use 110
Past participle, verbs 35
Periodic sentence structure 130
Personality, effect on tone 119
  in style 126
Personal pronouns, use of 115
Personification 100
Perspective, in logic 89
Persuasive organization 82
Persuasiveness
  importance of 4
  in writing 95
  objectives for achieving 95
  what it means 54
Phrases
  types of 23
  what they are 16, 21
Placement of modifiers, for
  emphasis 114
Poetic writing, avoid 133
Point of view, importance of clarity 82
Pompous prose 101, 122
Positive form, saves words 142
  in emphasis 113
Practice, to improve 151
Predicate, of sentence 13
Prepositions, use 15
Presentation formats 75
Projection, into audience 150
Pronouns
  can save words 140
  improper case 37
  relative 24
  remote reference 41, 96
  use of 41

Psychology of argument 83
Punctuation, use and misuse 31
Pyramid, logic concept 82

Qualifications, causes wordiness 136
Question mark (?), use of 31

Readibility 121
Redundencies 142
Relative pronouns 24
Report, format 73
Rereading, importance of ... 49, 149
Respect, for audience 120
Restrictive clauses and phrases .. 32
Rythm
  for style 129
  of sentence 130
  through voice 112

Semantics
  what it is.................... 99
  saves words 139
Semicolon (;), use of 34
Sentence, definition of 13
  types of 25
  fragments 45
Sight recognition of words 29
Simile 100
Simple sentence 25
Simple writing, importance of .. 135
Slang 43
Slide format 75
Sound
  grammar school 122
  of writing 118
  pompous prose 122
Spelling
  importance of 27
  phoenetic mistakes 27
  pronunciation 27
  rules 29
  transposition mistakes 27
  word usage 28
Split infinitives 46
Style
  reflection of personality 126
  through control 127
  through good grammar 128
                        (continued)

Style   (continued)
  through rythm 129
  through vocabulary 130
  what it is 125
Subject, of sentence 13

Tailoring style 134
Technical words, use of 133
Technology, in communications .. 62
Tense
  shifts in 37
  of verbs 37
Text book format 75
"Than," check for complete
  comparison 45
"That," leave out at your own risk 45
"There," proper use of 141
Thesaurus, used for 43
Thesis, in an essay 73
"This," use of, caution flag 96
Thought grouping, hierarchy
  concept 20
"To," use as a preposition versus
  use as an infinitive 21
  at end of sentence for emphasis 114
Tone
  through semantics 118
  types of 117
  what it is 118
Tongue twisters 133
Trite expressions 132
"Type of" habit 132

Uncertainty, in tone 120
Unity, of paragraphs 86
Unnecessary introductions 142

Variety, in style 129
Verbals, what they are 19
Verbs 13
Vocabulary, importance of 43
Voice
  active or passive 39, 109
  how formed 39
  use of 109

Weighting, of an argument 84
"Who, whom," usage 41
Windy phrases 141

Wordiness, unnecessary 136
Words
  misunderstood 43
  misused through carelessness .. 43
Worthless qualifiers 142
Writing
  objectives achieve business
    objectives 53
  reflection of the individual 12
  talent is a rarity 1
Writing objectives, understanding
  is prerequisite for effective
  communications 5